WORKHOUSES
OF THE NORTH

T0322559

Henry VIII's dissolution of the monasteries in 1536-39 also contributed to the problem. The monasteries had not only provided much direct or indirect employment, but had also been a significant source of alms to those in need. Such factors contributed to a substantial increase in the number of unemployed men roaming around the country in search of work and, if they could not find it, turning to vagrancy and begging.

Various parliamentary Acts were passed during the 1500s which aimed to curb begging and also to place on local parishes the responsibility for providing relief to the deserving or 'impotent' poor – those who could not work due to old age, sickness etc. An Act of 1536 required churchwardens to collect voluntary alms both to relieve the poor, sick and needy, and to set to work 'sturdy and idle vagabonds and valiant beggars'. Begging was always treated as a serious offence and in 1547 the Statute of Legal Settlement enacted that a sturdy beggar could be branded or made a slave for two years (or for life if he absconded). The same Act condemned any 'foolish pity and mercy' for vagrants, but for the impotent poor it proposed that cottages were to be erected for their habitation, and that they should be relieved or cured. In 1563, the contributions to parish funds by householders for poor relief became compulsory rather than voluntary. A further Act in 1576 stipulated that every town should set up stocks of materials (wool, flax, hemp, iron etc.) for the unemployed able-bodied poor to work on, either in their own homes or in a workshop. Every county was also to set up a punitive House of Correction for dealing with any able-bodied pauper who refused to work.

THE OLD POOR LAW

Elements from these earlier statutes were brought together in 1597 in an Act for the Relief of the Poor, re-enacted in a slightly revised form in 1601. The 1601 Act, the cornerstone of what became known as the Old Poor Law, laid down that the parish was the body responsible for poor relief, and that relief was to be funded by the local poor rate raised from householders. Materials were to be bought to set the able-bodied poor to work (with the threat of the House of Correction for anyone refusing to do so), while 'houses of dwelling' could be set up for the impotent poor.

The poor rate was collected by a parish official called an overseer (an unpaid and often unpopular post) and administered by the parish Vestry (a committee comprising the minister, churchwardens and a number of householders). Most parish poor relief was distributed as 'out-relief' – handouts in the form of money, food, fuel and clothing, to people living in their own homes.

Although the 1601 Act talked about 'work' and 'houses', it did not mention 'workhouses' – establishments which provided accommodation for the poor and where work had to be performed by those inmates who were able to do so.

EARLY WORKHOUSES

The earliest workhouses, such as one set up in York in 1567, were more like what we would now call workshops, that is, non-residential establishments where raw materials such as wool, hemp, flax or iron were supplied to provide work and training to the poor. At Sheffield, the Corporation's accounts from 1628 onwards record that they spent around £200 on the erection of a workhouse together with a stock of raw materials for providing employment. Eight shillings was spent on 'the carpenters' charges going to Newarke to see their workhouse'. Another early establishment was in Halifax, which in 1635 was granted a charter by Charles to set up a workhouse. Gradually, the idea evolved of providing the poor with both work and lodging in a single establishment, often with the former being required in return for the latter.

Although the words workhouse and poorhouse are often used interchangeably, the term poorhouse can sometimes denote an establishment, often for the elderly, where work was not required and a kinder regime operated, for example where there was no resident Master and no prescribed diet. Another point of terminology of particular relevance to the north of England concerns the term 'parish'. Northern parishes often covered a large area within which several centres of population, or 'townships', were located. From 1662, such townships were put on a par with parishes for the purposes of poor relief.

SETTLEMENT

The 1662 Settlement Act spelled out who a parish or township was responsible for − namely, those who could claim 'settlement' there. A child's settlement at birth was taken to be the same as that of its father. At marriage, a woman took on the same settlement as her husband. Illegitimate children were granted settlement in the place they were born − this often led parish overseers to try and get rid of an unmarried pregnant woman before the child was born, for example by transporting her to another parish just before the birth, or by paying a man from another parish to marry her.

Settlement could also be acquired in various ways, for example by renting a property for at least £10 a year, but this was well beyond the means of an average labourer. If a boy became apprenticed, which could happen from the age of seven, his parish of settlement became the place of his apprenticeship. Another means of qualifying for settlement in a new parish was by being in continuous employment for at least a year. To prevent this, hirings were often for a period of 364 days rather than a full year. On the other hand, labourers might quit their jobs before a year was up in order to avoid being trapped in a disagreeable parish.

CIVIC INCORPORATIONS

In 1696, Bristol promoted its own local Act of Parliament enabling it to set up a corporation for the management of poor relief, including the establishment of a workhouse. More than thirty large towns eventually went down this path beginning in 1698 with Colchester, Crediton, Exeter, Hereford, Shaftesbury, Tiverton, and − one of the few northern towns to be so incorporated − Kingston-upon-Hull.

Hull's Corporation workhouse, located on Whitefriargate, was known as Charity Hall. The Corporation comprised the town's Mayor, Recorder, twelve Aldermen, and twenty-four other inhabitants. However, the initial scheme was apparently not a success and the workhouse proved 'almost useless', being used instead for the next thirty years as a training school and home for pauper children. Early urban workhouses often targeted pauper children as a group likely to be in need of care, but who could be usefully trained and perform work to contribute towards their maintenance.

THE WORKHOUSE TEST

The early 1700s saw a growing use of the workhouse by parishes to try and limit the growing demand on the poor rate. This was achieved in two ways. First of all, placing paupers together in a single house could in itself save money compared with providing food, heating and rent for a large number of people in their own homes. Second, a parish could decide to make the workhouse the only form of relief it was prepared to offer in the hope that this would deter spurious claims. Anyone who was prepared to suffer entry into the workhouse could be judged worthy of sufficient need. In 1723, this so-called 'workhouse test' became incorporated into Knatchbull's Act which provided a clearer framework for parishes to set up and operate a workhouse.

Knatchbull's Act also allowed parishes to contract-out the time-consuming business of running a workhouse, a procedure which became known as 'farming' the poor. The contractor

IMAGES OF ENGLAND

WORKHOUSES
OF THE NORTH

PETER HIGGINBOTHAM

Frontispiece: The main block of Sheffield's Fir Vale workhouse in around 1900.

First published in 2006 by Tempus Publishing
Reprinted in 2007

Reprinted in 2009 by
The History Press
The Mill, Brimscombe Port,
Stroud, Gloucestershire, GL5 2QG
www.thehistorypress.co.uk

Reprinted 2011, 2012

British Library Cataloguing in Publication Data.
A catalogue record for this book is available from the British Library.

ISBN 978 0 7524 4001 9

Typesetting and origination by
Tempus Publishing Limited.
Printed in Great Britain.

CONTENTS

ACKNOWLEDGEMENTS

Permission to use the following pictures has very kindly been granted by: Liverpool Record Office for photographs of the Brownlow Hill, Toxteth Park and Walton-on-the-Hill workhouses, and the Fazakerley Cottage Homes; St James' Hospital, Leeds, for the photograph of the Leeds female inmates; Doncaster Library and Information Services for the photographs of the Doncaster workhouses; Pamela Repussard for the archive photographs of Sheffield's Fir Vale.

The Poor Law Union maps are based on data from: Southall, H.R., Gilbert, D.R., Gregory, I., Furnis, P. *Great Britain Historical Database Online, 1841-1939* [computer file]. Colchester, Essex: AHDS History, UK Data Archive [distributor], 23 March 2000. SN: 33305.

Opposite above: Oakum picking – the teasing-out of old ropes into their raw fibres – was a task frequently given to workhouse inmates. The resulting material was sold to ship-builders who mixed it with tar to seal the lining of wooden ships.

Opposite below: The spacious interior of Fir Vale kitchens, *c.* 1902. The cook is carving a large turkey, so this may indeed be 'Christmas day in the workhouse'.

INTRODUCTION

THE SHAME OF THE WORKHOUSE

The workhouse is an institution which, perhaps more than any other, has left a deep emotional scar on the British nation. Even today, three quarters of a century after the workhouse system was officially abolished in 1930, many older people still remember being told as children to 'behave or you'll end up in the workhouse'. Some local hospitals that were former workhouses still carry the taint of their past, with elderly patients reluctant to countenance entry into the place they still think of as 'where people go to die'. Even where the connection is much more distant, the workhouse can still cast its shadow – for example, in Kendal, a street sign for 'ANCHORITE PLACE formerly Poorhouse Lane' has had the second part whitewashed out, presumably because of its uncomfortable associations.

The shame of the workhouse was acknowledged in official circles in 1904 when the Registrar General issued a recommendation to local registrars that children born in workhouses should not be identifiable from their birth certificates because of the stigma this would carry in later life. In such cases, a euphemistic address was recorded as the place of birth. For example, the Liverpool Union workhouse was thereafter referred to on such certificates simply as '144A Brownlow Hill' although no such street address actually existed.

Despite the emotions that the workhouse can still evoke, its study can often illuminate our understanding of the broader social, political, economic, medical and architectural history of Britain, both at the national and local level. People are often surprised to discover that a former workhouse building still exists in their locality. Regrettably, though, the stock of surviving examples continues to decline under the pressure of redevelopment. Family historians, too, who discover a workhouse connection on a birth or death certificate, can often experience a real sense of connection with their past by seeing, or even visiting first-hand, the building in question.

Using a mixture of vintage and modern images, this book takes a look at some of these influential buildings within whose walls degradation and misery was so often to be found. This volume focuses on the northern part of England covering the old counties of Cumberland, Durham, Lancashire, Northumberland, Westmorland, and Yorkshire.

THE ORIGINS OF THE WORKHOUSE

The workhouse had its roots in Tudor times and its development forms part of the much larger story of how state-organised relief was administered to the poor and destitute over the following four centuries.

The sixteenth century in England was a time of great social and economic change. In the countryside, arable land was increasingly being converted to pasture, resulting in a reduction in the amount of agricultural labour required. The expansion of towns, particularly those involved in textile manufacturing, resulted in a rising influx of workers from outside. However, this meant a correspondingly high level of destitution in periodic times of manufacturing depression.

Hull's Charity Hall – a large U-shaped building, three storeys high plus attics, which could hold up to 180 inmates.

would provide premises, perhaps in a rented house, and maintain its inmates with board, lodging and work. In return he would receive a weekly or annual sum from the parish, together with any income generated from the paupers' work.

THE WORKHOUSE BOOM

In the wake of Knatchbull's Act, there was a boom in the opening of parish workhouses, with as many as 700 estimated to have been in operation by 1732. The use of workhouses was also espoused by the Quakers who ran their own workhouse in Clerkenwell from 1702, and the Society for the Promotion of Christian Knowledge (SPCK) who published literature giving advice on workhouse operation such as recommendations for Masters, guides to rules and diets etc. The most influential of these works was *An Account of Several Work-houses for Employing and Maintaining the Poor* published in 1725. The *Account* catalogued 126 establishments, while an enlarged edition of 1732 added a further fifty-five. Only four of the entries were located in the northern counties: Ashton-under-Lyne and Warrington in Lancashire, and Beverley and Kingston-upon-Hull in Yorkshire. This may, however, reflect the *Account*'s southern bias rather than a real dearth of workhouses in the north.

Beverley's parish workhouse, with a capacity of 100 inmates, opened in Midsummer 1727. The application of the workhouse test initially had a dramatic effect on the numbers of applicants for relief, reducing it from 116 to twenty-six. Beverley's paupers were also required to wear 'the Badge'. Badging the poor had been introduced by an Act of 1697 whereby anyone in receipt of poor relief could be required to wear, on their sleeve or shoulder, a badge in red or blue cloth containing the initial letter of the parish followed by a letter 'P' (for parish) e.g. BP for Beverley Parish.

The *Abstract of Returns Made by the Overseers of the Poor* published by Parliament in 1776-7 recorded over 1,800 workhouses in operation – almost one for every seven parishes in England and Wales. In the north, there were fifty-three in Lancashire, 152 in Yorkshire, and a combined total of 119 for Cumberland, Durham, Northumberland, and Westmorland.

Many local workhouses during this period were modest affairs, able to accommodate perhaps ten or twenty inmates. Some, such as Chapel Allerton, provided a roof for only two. The

HOUSE OF INDUSTRY.

Liverpool's House of Industry on Brownlow Hill, erected in 1769-72, formed the heart of England's largest workhouse, which eventually grew to accommodate over 5,000 inmates.

larger industrial towns such as Sheffield, Manchester, Wigan, Hull and Leeds had much larger establishments catering for up to 200. Liverpool had a massive 600 places.

GILBERT'S ACT

Another impetus to the setting up of workhouses came in 1782 with the passing of an Act 'For the Better Relief and Employment of the Poor', better known as Gilbert's Act after its promoter Thomas Gilbert. The Act encouraged groups or 'unions' of parishes to set up a common workhouse for the old, the sick and infirm, and orphan children. Able-bodied paupers were not to be admitted but instead found employment near their own homes, with employers receiving allowances from the poor rates to bring wages up to subsistence levels. Gilbert's Act also improved the administration of poor relief and provided model rules for the running of a workhouse. Unions were controlled by a board of Guardians, one from each member parish. However, Gilbert's scheme never became widely adopted and less than a hundred Gilbert Unions were ever formed. Those in the north included:

Cumberland:	Whitehaven
Durham:	Darlington
Lancashire:	Caton
Westmorland:	Eamont Bridge, Kirkby Lonsdale, Kirkby Stephen, Milnthorpe
Yorkshire:	Bainbridge, Barwick, Bolton-by-Bowland, Carlton, Giggleswick, Great Ouseburn, Lawkland, Leyburn, Lockington, Paghill or Paul, Great Preston, Saddleworth

Amongst the largest Gilbert Unions were those in the West Riding of Yorkshire, with the Barwick, Carlton, Great Ouseburn and Great Preston Unions reaching a membership of forty parishes or more.

THE STATE OF THE POOR

A comprehensive picture of workhouse operation in the 1790s is provided by Sir Frederic Eden's massive work *The State of the Poor* published in 1797. Its three volumes contain detailed reports from over 170 parishes throughout England and Wales. Here is part of Eden's description of the Liverpool 'House of Industry', erected in 1769-72 at Brownlow Hill, and by now containing 1,220 of the town's poor:

> The most infirm live on the ground floor; others are distributed through the upper storeys. They all dine together in a large room, which occasionally serves as a chapel. The children are mostly employed in picking cotton, but are too crowded, 70 or 80 working in a small room. About 50 girls are bound apprentices in sprigging muslin. The house receives from 1s. to 2s. 6d. a week for each. A few old men are employed in boat building. Tailors and other trades are carried on in the house. The annual expense of a pauper in the Liverpool Workhouse does not exceed £7, which may be considered moderate when compared with the heavy charges in other parts of England. Weekly bill of fare: Breakfast, every day–Oatmeal, hasty pudding, known as burgo, and milk. Dinner–Monday, Friday–Milk pottage and bread; Tuesday, Thursday, Saturday–Lobscouse, i.e. beef cut into small pieces and boiled with potatoes; Wednesday, Sunday–Broth, beef and bread. Supper–Monday, Tuesday, Saturday–Milk pottage and bread; Wednesday, Sunday–Broth, beef and bread; Thursday, Friday–Milk and bread. The bread is household bread. According to the table of expenses, 142½ lbs. of ale and beer at 1d. per lb. are consumed every day, and about 434 gallons of sweet milk (at 8 lbs. to the gallon) every week. About 2,700 out pensioners are also relieved, at a weekly expense of £56 9s. The committee refuse relief to such Poor as keep dogs.

Hasty pudding – milk boiled up with flour or oatmeal – was also on the menu at Kendal and Kirkland in Westmorland. Its house rules stipulated that 'no person be allowed to smoke in their bed, or in their rooms, upon pain of being put six hours in the dungeon.' Failure to wear the paupers' badge marked KKP (Kendal and Kirkland Parish) would result in four hours in the dungeon. Anyone convicted of lying would be made to stand on a stool 'in the most public place of the dining room, while the rest are at dinner, and have papers fixed on their breasts, with these words written thereon, INFAMOUS LYAR, and shall loose that meal.'

THE END OF THE OLD POOR LAW

The early decades of the nineteenth century saw a time of crisis in the poor relief system. The end of the Napoleonic wars in 1815, together with the corn laws, which restricted the import of cheap foreign grain, led to high food prices, unemployment and a downturn in the economy. In many parts of the country, the supplementing of labourers' wages from the poor rate, recommended by Gilbert's Act, had become widespread. The practice had become formalised in 1795 in the so-called Speenhamland system which linked wage supplements to the price of bread and size of family.

As a result of these factors, the national cost of poor relief rose enormously – from around £1.5 million in 1776, to a peak of £7.87 million in 1818. In parish after parish across the country, the escalating cost of the poor rates appeared to be unstoppable.

A few places, however, managed to buck the national trend. In the parishes of Bingham and Southwell in Nottinghamshire, experiments were taking place with a new regime of poor relief. At Southwell in the early 1820s, George Nicholls, a retired sea-captain who had become an honorary overseer of the poor in the parish, virtually abolished out-relief and instead offered claimants only the workhouse. The workhouse was strictly and economically run, with males

The Bainbridge Gilbert Union workhouse, later used as the Aysgarth Union workhouse. This sturdy Yorkshire building reaches its second centenary in 2013.

and females segregated, work required of the inmates, and a restricted diet. As a result, the parish's poor relief expenditure fell from £1,884 in 1821-2 to £811 in the following year. In 1824, a much larger workhouse run on similar lines was opened nearby by the Thurgarton Hundred Incorporation, again achieving significant financial savings.

Elsewhere in the country, discontent amongst the labouring classes reached a climax in the autumn of 1830 when agricultural labourers across southern England protested against low wages, expensive food and the growing mechanization of farms. Threatening letters sent to land-owners and farmers were signed 'Swing' – the supposed, although probably fictitious, leader of the protests. Workhouses were amongst the rioters' targets – on 22 November a mob in Hampshire ransacked the Selborne parish workhouse. The following day, an even larger mob, including the Selborne rioters, did the same to the workhouse at nearby Headley. The ringleaders were later transported to Australia.

There was discontent, too, amongst the electorate – the landed classes who were footing the bill for the spiralling poor rates, and for whom the possibility of further civil unrest was highly disturbing.

THE ROYAL COMMISSION OF 1832

In the spring of 1832, the government set up a Royal Commission to conduct a detailed survey of the state of poor law administration. A team of twenty-six Assistant Commissioners was assembled to collect information from around 3,000 (approximately one in five) of the parishes in England and Wales.

The Commission's report, issued in 1834, contained a series of twenty-two recommendations which were to form the basis of the new legislation that followed in the same year. The main proposals were:

- The end of relief to the able-bodied except through 'well-regulated workhouses'
- That workhouse conditions be no better than those of the lowest independent labourer

Opened in 1824, the Thurgarton Hundred Incorporation workhouse accommodated 158 inmates. The building had segregated sections for males and females, and for the infirm and the able-bodied. Its design was a major influence on later workhouses.

- The grouping of parishes for the purposes of operating a workhouse
- The appointment of a central body to administer the new system

THE NEW POOR LAW

The 1834 Act for the Amendment and better Administration of the Laws relating to the Poor in England and Wales became known as the 'New Poor Law'. The new system, unlike its predecessors, was to be compulsory, and operate in a uniform manner across the whole of England and Wales.

The Act itself was largely concerned with setting up a new administrative framework under which the new system of poor relief was to be administered. It created a new all-powerful central administrative body called the Poor Law Commissioners (PLC) based at Somerset House in London. The three Commissioners appointed were George Nicholls, John Shaw-Lefevre and Thomas Frankland Lewis. Edwin Chadwick became the Commissioners' Secretary.

At the local level, the 15,000 or so parishes in England and Wales were divided into new administrative units called poor law unions. A union typically contained twenty or thirty parishes or townships and was run by a Board of Guardians elected by the local rate-payers. Each union was required to provide workhouse accommodation for its poor to meet the requirements of the new Act. Local Act Incorporations and Gilbert Unions were exempted from the new scheme, something that was to prove an irritation to the Commissioners and their successors for many years.

The funding of each union and its workhouse continued to come from the local poor rate. Each parish contributed in proportion to its average poor relief expenditure over the previous three years. This meant that the greatest share was generally paid by parishes with the highest numbers of paupers rather those with the wealthiest ratepayers.

The Act did not go into the practical details of how the new poor relief administration was to operate. The detailed policy and implementation of the new system came through the large volume of orders and regulations issued by the PLC which specified every aspect of the operation of a union and its workhouse.

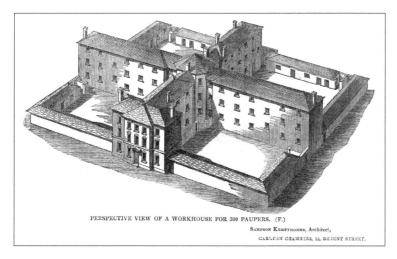

PERSPECTIVE VIEW OF A WORKHOUSE FOR 300 PAUPERS. (F.)

Sampson Kempthorne, Architect,
CARLTON CHAMBERS, 12, REGENT STREET.

A perspective view of Sampson Kempthorne's model 'square' design – one of the most popular early workhouse layouts. Critics of the New Poor Law likened it to prison designs of the time, disparagingly referring to it as a 'Bastille' after the large prison in Paris.

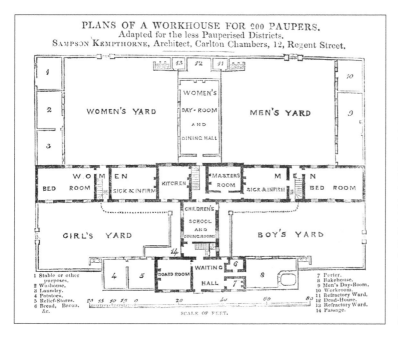

Northern unions that did build new workhouses were more likely to adopt designs based on Kempthorne's '200-pauper' plan which lacked the supervisory hub. The wash-house and laundry were placed on the women's side, while the men's side had a workroom. Refractory wards, for confining those who misbehaved, were next to the mortuary.

One of the PLC's first tasks was to organise the setting up of the new poor law unions. An Assistant Poor Law Commissioner was appointed to each area and visited each proposed union to meet with its 'respectable inhabitants', examine the existing levels of parish poor rates and workhouse accommodation etc., and to advise on the procedure for setting up the union and the election of its Board of Guardians.

The Board of Guardians met weekly to carry out the business of the union. Their first meeting would generally include the election of a Chairman and appointment of a Clerk and Treasurer. The next most important item for attention would then be the provision of workhouse accommodation.

CLASSIFICATION AND SEGREGATION

A basic principle of the new system was the classification of paupers into different categories (male/female, infirm/able-bodied, and so on). Separate accommodation was to be provided for each category with no contact between them. If an able-bodied man entered the workhouse, he had to take his whole family with him with the family being separated up as soon as they were admitted. Conversely, the whole family had to leave together – so that a husband could not abandon his family in the workhouse.

The 1832 Royal Commission had originally proposed that each union should operate separate workhouses for different categories of pauper inmate: 'At least four classes are necessary:– 1. The aged and really impotent; 2. The children; 3. The able-bodied females; 4. The able-bodied males.' Apart from providing different types of accommodation to suit the particular needs of different groups, separate establishments would also have allowed many former parish workhouses to be reused under the new system. However, running four or more institutions for unpredictable numbers of inmates soon began to look expensive and difficult, especially when it came to dispersing and reuniting families entering or leaving the workhouse. Thus most unions adopted the 'general mixed workhouse' as the single workhouse for the whole union.

The PLC devised the following sevenfold classification of workhouse inmates, each of which was to be housed separately:

1. Aged or infirm men
2. Able-bodied men, and youths above thirteen
3. Youths and boys above seven years old and under thirteen
4. Aged or infirm women
5. Able-bodied women and girls above sixteen
6. Girls above seven years old and under sixteen
7. Children under seven years of age

In fact, there were some exceptions to the segregation rule. Children under seven could be placed (if the Guardians thought fit) in the female quarters and, from 1842, their mothers could have access to them 'at all reasonable times'. Parents could also have an 'interview' with their children 'at some time in each day'. From 1847, married couples over the age of sixty could request a shared bedroom, although few unions provided this facility.

WORKHOUSE BUILDINGS

In providing workhouse accommodation, unions were faced with the choice of enlarging and adapting existing workhouse buildings, or staring from scratch with a completely new purpose-built workhouse. Between 1835 and 1839, over half of the 583 Boards of Guardians in England and Wales opted for the latter course.

The new workhouses had to fulfil a number of very specific requirements, one of the uppermost being the easy segregation of the different classes of inmate. Another of the aims of the new system was that the operation of poor relief should be uniform across the country. In 1835, to help unions meet these requirements, the PLC published a number of model workhouse plans, most of which were designed by a young architect called Sampson Kempthorne whose father was a friend of the Poor Law Commissioner, George Nicholls. Kempthorne's most influential design was known as the cruciform or square layout.

At the front was an entrance block containing a porter's room and waiting room on the ground floor, with the Guardians' board-room above. To the rear were a children's school and dining room, connecting to the central supervision hub of the workhouse where the workhouse Master had his quarters. From the hub radiated a women's wing to the left and a men's wing to the right, each being divided into separate sections for the able-bodied and for the elderly and infirm. Day rooms occupied the ground floor of each wing, and dormitories the upper floor. A fourth wing contained the workhouse kitchens, scullery, larder, stores etc. with a combined dining-hall and chapel above. The area between the wings formed exercise yards were often further subdivided by walls to create separate areas for the different classes. The upper floors of the hub had windows in each direction giving a view over all the yards.

Despite their popularity elsewhere in the country, only a handful of northern unions, such as Ulverston and Ormskirk, erected workhouses based on Kempthorne's initial designs. A few others, such as Thorne and Wigton, opted for plans based on his smaller and cheaper 'Workhouse for 200 Paupers Adapted for the Less Pauperised Districts' published by the PLC in 1836.

RESISTANCE TO THE NEW LAW

Through 1835 and 1836, the unionization of the southern counties of England proceeded relatively smoothly, with only one or two isolated and short-lived outbreaks of resistance. In the north of England, however, the 1834 Act met with considerable opposition. This was particularly strong in the textile manufacturing areas of north-eastern Lancashire and west Yorkshire such as Oldham, Rochdale and Huddersfield.

Resistance came partly from the labouring classes, led by men such as Richard Oastler, who had gained valuable experience of organising protests while campaigning to improve factory conditions. There was also hostility from the local landowners and ratepayers whose cooperation was required to operate the new system. During periods of manufacturing slump, the traditional approach to poor relief in many industrial towns had been to give short-term handouts to unemployed workers who were suffering hardship. A new workhouse was seen as a wasteful expense that would involve large capital expenditure, spend most of its time empty, and which would in any case be unable to cope with the large numbers of relief claimants during periodic downturns. Giving a short-term dole to a worker was viewed as much preferable to having to maintain a whole family in the workhouse.

One of the first northern protests took place in Huddersfield in December 1836. News of the imminent introduction on the New Poor Law in the town provoked a demonstration by 8,000 people in the marketplace at the end of which an effigy of a Poor Law Commissioner was burned.

Opposition took a variety of forms including the boycotting of Guardians' elections, the withholding of poor law rates, and the refusal of Boards of Guardians to elect officers or conduct union business. On a number of occasions, violence erupted with police and even armed cavalry having to be called in to restore order. Another tactic was non-cooperation with the Assistant Poor Law Commissioner for the region, Alfred Power. Power's frequent heavy-handedness in dealing with antagonistic Boards of Guardians undoubtedly also aggravated matters.

In 1841, the PLC issued a General Order for the Prohibition of Outdoor Relief, supposedly setting the seal on their determination to end out-relief to the able-bodied. However, in face of sustained northern opposition, the Commissioners were already being forced to make concessions. From 1837 onwards, individual unions could be issued with a Labour Test Order which permitted out-relief to be given to able-bodied men in return for manual labour such as stone breaking. Many northern unions exploited the General Order's list of permitted exceptions and issued outdoor relief under the guise of it being medical relief or 'sudden and urgent necessity'.

A final obstacle to the progress of unionization was the continuing existence of Gilbert Unions – this was a particular problem in West Yorkshire where four Gilbert Unions survived to disrupt the Commissioners' unionization efforts.

As far as workhouse provision was concerned, it was common for northern unions to retain one or more former parish or township workhouses. In Cumberland and Westmorland, for example, only three of the twelve new unions erected new workhouses, while only two of Lancashire's original twenty-five poor law unions initially did so. Unfortunately for their inmates, many of the old buildings were cramped, dirty, badly ventilated, and with poor sanitation. Under continuing pressure from the PLC, and their successors, the Poor Law Board, most northern unions had erected new purpose-built workhouses by the 1870s. Among the last to do so was Todmorden, which had steadfastly refused to provide any new workhouse accommodation. It was only under the threat of dissolution that the union finally capitulated in 1877.

Unlike the plain and forbidding workhouse designs of the 1830s, many of the new northern workhouses erected in the 1850s and 1860s were impressive buildings, often designed in the fashionable architectural style of the day. Like other civic buildings of the era, workhouses could reflect a town's growing prosperity and visibly demonstrate what it was prepared to spend on providing for its poor. The erection of a workhouse often brought about a change in attitude amongst the Board of Guardians, and also an increase in their local standing as managers of a now large and impressive institution.

WORKHOUSE LIFE

On entering the workhouse, new inmates usually spent some time in a receiving ward where they received a medical inspection. They were given a bath, had their own clothes taken away for disinfecting and storage, and were issued with the workhouse uniform. For men this was typically a jacket and trousers made in rough cloth, striped cotton shirt, cloth cap and shoes. A common women's uniform was a shapeless, waistless, blue-and-white-striped shift-frock reaching to the ankles, with a smock over. Old women wore a bonnet or mop-cap, shawl, and apron over.

The daily life of the workhouse was conducted to the timetable shown below, which was punctuated by the ringing of the workhouse bell. On Sundays, no work was performed except for essential domestic chores.

	Rise	Breakfast	Start work	Dinner	End work	Supper	Bedtime
25 March to 29 September	6am	6.30-7am	7am	12-1pm	6pm	6-7pm	8pm
29 September to 25 March	7am	7.30-8am	8am	12-1pm	6pm	6-7pm	8pm

Communal prayers were read before breakfast and after supper every day and Divine Service performed on Sunday, Good Friday and Christmas Day. The rules demanded that during meals 'silence, order and decorum shall be maintained', although from 1842 the word 'silence' was dropped.

In 1836, the Poor Law Commissioners issued six standard dietaries which varied slightly in the amount and composition of food they provided. Each union chose the one it felt most suitable for its own workhouse. Other variations could be adopted with the approval of the PLC. On admission, each inmate was allocated to a particular dietary class which varied in amount and 'extras'. In 1847, the dietary classes were: 1. Able-bodied Men; 2. Old and Infirm Men; 3. Boys from nine to sixteen; 4. Boys from two to nine; 5. Able-bodied Women; 6. Old and Infirm Women; 7. Girls from nine to sixteen; 8. Girls from two to nine; 9. Infants.

Preston's Watling Street workhouse, erected in 1865–8, was typical of the turnaround in several industrial northern unions in the 1850s and 1860s. Years of resisting the 1834 Act, and clinging on to old and inadequate township workhouses, were replaced by lavish spending.

An example of able-bodied women inmates' workhouse uniform. This striking picture was taken at the Leeds workhouse in the 1920s.

The type of work demanded from the able-bodied inmates was largely at the discretion of the local Guardians. Some workhouses had workshops for sewing, spinning and weaving or other local trades. Others had their own vegetable gardens where the inmates worked to provide food for the workhouse. Women performed the domestic tasks of cooking, cleaning, and the workhouse laundry. Men were given heavy manual work such as:

- Stone-breaking – the results were saleable for road-making
- Corn-grinding – heavy mill-stones were rotated by four or more men turning a capstan (the resulting flour was usually of very poor quality)
- Gypsum-crushing – for use in plaster-making
- Oakum-picking – teasing out the fibres from old hemp ropes
- Bone-crushing – old bones were pulverised to produce fertiliser

Bone-crushing was abolished after a much publicised scandal at Andover workhouse in 1845 where the diet was so poor that men were found to have been fighting over shreds of rotting meat left on the bones they had been set to crush. The scandal was instrumental in the PLC being replaced in 1847 by the new Poor Law Board which was more directly accountable to Parliament.

Workhouse discipline distinguished two classes of offence. Disorderly conduct, which included swearing, failing to wash, refusing to work, playing cards, or feigning sickness could be punished by a withdrawal of food 'luxuries' such as cheese or tea. The more serious category of Refractory conduct, such as disobeying or insulting a workhouse officer, being drunk, or damaging workhouse property, could result in a period of solitary confinement. More serious misdemeanours could be referred to a magistrate – an act such as deliberately breaking a window could result in two months' prison and hard labour.

Another serious offence was the stealing of union property – this included the workhouse uniform. Although an inmate could discharge himself from the workhouse at any time – workhouses were not prisons – he could not just walk out of the door. A few hours' notice had to be given for his own clothes to be retrieved.

CHILDREN IN THE WORKHOUSE
After 1834, Poor Law Unions were required to provide at least three hours a day of schooling for workhouse children. Children were to be taught 'reading, writing, arithmetic, and the principles of the Christian Religion, and such other instruction as may fit them for service, and train them to habits of usefulness, industry and virtue.' By the 1840s, unions were being encouraged to place children in buildings separate from the workhouse to remove them from any polluting association with the adult workhouse inmates. A variety of establishments evolved to perform this role:

- **District Schools**. Amongst the first to adopt the separation policy was Manchester which, in 1843, erected a large school at Swinton. In 1845, Liverpool opened a large Industrial School at Kirkdale which, by 1850, had over 1,100 children in residence. Pupils were taught trades to equip them for later life. For boys, these included tailoring, shoemaking and carpentry. For boys with a sea-going inclination, Kirkdale erected a 'ship' in its grounds and employed an old sailor to teach nautical skills. Girls were instructed in knitting and needlework, washing, ironing, mangling and cooking, to qualify them for domestic service. District Schools (known disparagingly as Barrack Schools) were often a breeding ground for infectious diseases such as ophthalmia and ringworm.

No. 3.—DIETARY for ABLE-BODIED PAUPERS.	BREAKFAST.		DINNER.					SUPPER.	
	Bread.	Gruel.	Cooked Meat.	Potatoes or other Vegetables.	Soup.	Bread.	Cheese.	Bread.	Cheese.
	oz.	pints.	oz.	lb.	pints.	oz.	oz.	oz.	oz.
Sunday . . Men .	8	1½	. .	. .	. .	7	2	6	1½
Women	6	1½	. .	.	.	6	1½	5	1½
Monday . . Men .	8	1½	. .	.	.	7	2	6	1½
Women	6	1½	. .	.	.	6	1½	5	1½
Tuesday . . Men .	8	1½	8	¾	. .	. .	.	6	1½
Women	6	1½	6	¾	. .	. .	.	5	1½
Wednesday . Men .	8	1½	. .	.	. .	7	2	6	1½
Women	6	1½	. .	.	. .	6	1½	5	1½
Thursday . . Men .	8	1½	. .	.	1½	6	.	6	1½
Women	6	1½	. .	.	1½	5	.	5	1½
Friday . . . Men .	8	1½	. .	.	. .	7	2	6	1½
Women	6	1½	. .	.	. .	6	1½	5	1½
Saturday . . Men .	8	1½	Bacon. 5	¾	. .	. .	. .	6	1½
Women	6	1½	4	¾	.	. .	. .	5	1½

Old people, of sixty years of age and upwards, may be allowed one ounce of tea, five ounces of butter, and seven ounces of sugar per week, in lieu of gruel for breakfast, if deemed expedient to make this change.

Children under nine years of age, to be dieted at discretion; above nine, to be allowed the same quantities as women.

Sick to be dieted as directed by the medical officer.

The No. 3 Dietary issued by the Poor Law Commissioners in 1836. After 1900, unions were free to devise their own dietaries.

• **Cottage Homes**. In the 1870s, some unions started experimenting with 'cottage homes' – a system pioneered in the 1850s at an agricultural colony for delinquent boys at Mettray in France. The homes, organised as 'family' groups of fifteen to twenty children plus a house-mother or father, proved successful in providing a remedial environment for juvenile offenders. Ideally, cottage homes were constructed as a self-contained 'village' in a rural location, typically with a dozen cottages plus a school, infirmary, administration and reception block, and even a swimming pool.

• **Scattered Homes**. In 1893, the system of isolated or 'scattered' homes was devised by J Wycliffe Wilson, Chairman of the Sheffield Guardians, who criticised cottage homes as isolating children from the real world. Scattered homes placed groups of children in ordinary domestic houses spread around the suburbs of towns such as Sheffield. Unlike cottage homes, children in scattered homes attended ordinary local schools. Otherwise, scattered homes were run much like cottage homes. Unions with many scattered homes usually erected a headquarters home to act as a receiving or probationary home for new arrivals.

• **Boarding Out**. This was a system for placing parentless children in the long-term care of foster parents who usually received a weekly allowance for each child staying with them. The system, which is usually said to have originated in Scotland, was seen as the nearest approximation to a 'normal' home life that could be provided by a union, and was also financially economical.

• **Training Ships**. A number of different organisations operated training ships which gave boys (or 'lads' as they were invariably known) aged from about twelve to sixteen, preparation for a life in the Royal or Merchant Navy. Some of these establishments, such as the *Indefatigable* anchored on the Mersey at New Ferry, Birkenhead, and the *Wellesley* at North Shields, took boys from poor law institutions.

THE END OF THE WORKHOUSE

The workhouse era ended, officially at least, on 1 April 1930; the 643 Boards of Guardians in England and Wales were abolished and their responsibilities passed to local authorities. Some workhouse buildings were sold off, demolished, or fell into disuse. Many, however, became Public

A workhouse dining-hall – its religious mottoes encouraging piety in those receiving relief.

Manchester's Swinton School was described in Charles Dickens' journal *Household Words* as 'a building which is generally mistaken for a wealthy nobleman's residence. The structure is not only elegant but extensive; it is in the Tudor style of architecture, with a frontage of four-hundred and fifty feet.' The building was demolished in the 1930s.

Newcastle Union's cottage homes for 300 children were erected in 1901 at Ponteland. Each cottage block housed between thirty and forty children supervised by a 'house-mother' and 'house-father'. The homes included a school, infirmary, workshops and a blacksmith's shop. The site is now the headquarters of Northumbria Police.

Assistance Institutions and continued to provide accommodation for the elderly, chronic sick, unmarried mothers and vagrants. For inmates of these institutions, life often changed relatively little during the 1930s and '40s. Apart from the abolition of uniforms, and more freedom to come and go, things improved only slowly. With the introduction of the National Health Service (NHS) in 1948, many former workhouse buildings continued to house the elderly and chronic sick. With the reorganisation of the NHS in the 1980s and '90s, the old buildings were often turned over for use as office space or demolished to make way for new hospital blocks or car parks. More recently, the survivors have increasingly been sold off for redevelopment, ironically, in some cases, as up-market residential accommodation.

WORKHOUSE DIRECTORY

The following sections present an alphabetical directory of workhouses in the north of England. Within each county, entries are organised by Poor Law Union – the main administrative unit for poor relief after 1834 – although in a few cases, Gilbert Unions or single Poor Law Parishes continued in this role. Where unions cross county borders, they are allocated to the county in which they were placed by the Poor Law authorities, usually the one where the largest proportion of their population lived.

Where possible, a National Grid Reference (e.g. SJ748784) is given to help identify the approximate modern location of each workhouse, either on a printed Ordnance Survey map, or via online mapping services such as Multimap (www.multimap.com) that allow a Grid Reference to be entered instead of a place name. Old maps showing workhouse locations can be found on the www.workhouses.org.uk and www.old-maps.co.uk websites.

A code at the end of each directory entry (e.g. CUC) indicates the record office where any surviving local records are to be found. A list of the codes is given at the end of the book.

CHAPTER I

CUMBERLAND

Longtown

Brampton

Carlisle

Wigton

Alston with
Garrigill

Penrith

Cockermouth

Whitehaven

Bootle

ALSTON WITH GARRIGILL

The isolated Alston with Garrigill parish workhouse (NY717460) probably dated from the mid-eighteenth century. In 1837, the building was adopted by new Alston with Garrigill Union. The workhouse comprised a block of four houses in a sloping terrace and accommodated up to eighty inmates although was rarely more than half full. Vagrants and receiving wards were provided in a separate block in the workhouse garden.

The buildings have now been converted to residential use. (CUC)

BOOTLE

The parishes of Bootle (not to be confused with its Merseyside namesake) and Millom had workhouses, both of which were taken over by the new Bootle Union in 1837.

A new union workhouse for 100 inmates was erected in 1856 at the west of Bootle (SD100884). According to an official inspection in 1866, 'employment and recreation are found for the males in the workhouse garden, and, for the women, in household work.'

The workhouse no longer exists but its former infirmary has been converted to a house. (CUW)

BRAMPTON

For nearly forty years, Brampton Union made do with its former parish workhouse located at the south of the town on Gelt Road (NY530605). Its ground-floor rooms were dark because of the wall which enclosed the site. The buildings still exist and have been converted to housing.

A new workhouse, now demolished, was built at the north of Brampton (NY530613) in 1875. It cost £15,000 and could house 200. It had an entrance block with central archway, behind which lay the T-shaped main building. An infirmary and isolation block stood at the north of the site. (CUC)

CARLISLE

The new Carlisle Union, formed in 1838, at first adopted three existing parish workhouses, with St Cuthbert's at Harraby Hill (NY411547) used for children, St Mary's on Devonshire Walk (NY396562) for the infirm, and Caldewgate at Bell Vue (NY374560) for the able-bodied.

The union opposed the New Poor Law, preferring to give short-term relief payments to workers during occasional downturns in trade. This, they argued, allowed them to carry on working rather than their whole family being expensively maintained in the workhouse. During a slump in 1839-40, 450 handloom weavers were suddenly in need of relief. Carlisle was one of the northern unions allowed to operate an 'outdoor labour test' where able-bodied men could be given outdoor relief as long as they performed hard manual labour such as stone-breaking in a specially set up labour yard. However, few were prepared to take this option and tried to scrape by as best they could. The plight of the weavers led to the setting up of charitable relief committees funded by local citizens.

Eventually, in 1863, a large new workhouse and infirmary were erected on Fusehill Street in Carlisle (NY409556). It could hold nearly 500 inmates.

In 1948, it became the City General Hospital. The site is now the University of Cumbria's Fusehill Campus. (CUC)

COCKERMOUTH

The Cockermouth Union erected a new workhouse on a site to the south of the Cockermouth between Gallowbarrow and Sullart Street (NY118304), with the first part opening in June 1841. Its original cost was £4,000 but an additional £500 was spent on improvements, with an

Alston with Garrigill's former workhouse. The remote location enjoys spectacular views over the South Tyne River.

additional east wing and fever hospital being added in 1847 at a cost of £600. The main building had a very similar layout to the nearby Penrith and Wigton workhouses, all being broadly based on Sampson Kempthorne's '200-pauper' model plan.

The workhouse closed in August 1935 and was used by the Royal Army Service Corps during the Second World War. The buildings were demolished in 1949.

In 1886, the union acquired premises at Flimby (NY025342) for conversion to a school and vagrant wards. (CUW)

LONGTOWN

In 1821, the parish of Arthuret erected a workhouse at the east of Longtown (NY410689). In 1837, the new Longtown Union took over and extended the Arthuret premises. The buildings comprised an entrance block and an inverted T-shaped main building. Water for the workhouse was supplied by a pump in the kitchen supplemented by water from a stream adjoining the premises. The 6 acres of grounds around the buildings were cultivated by the inmates.

The buildings no longer exist. (CUC)

PENRITH

Early workhouses existed at Middlegate in Penrith, at Heskett and at Ainstable.

In 1838, the new Penrith Union erected a workhouse on Greystoke Road, to the west of Penrith (NY504300) at a cost of around £3,000. Its design, like that of its neighbours at Wigton and Cockermouth, was based on the '200-pauper' model plan.

Only the hospital block, a later addition to the buildings, still survives — now converted to residential use. (CUC)

The casual ward of the Bootle workhouse, built in 1880 to deal with an increase in vagrants after a new ironworks was opened in the area.

Brampton's original parish workhouse which outlived the later union workhouse. It could house around eighty inmates. The block to the left was the workhouse hospital and infectious wards.

Carlisle's Fusehill Street workhouse site served as a military hospital during both world wars. It later became the City General Hospital, with the former workhouse infirmary becoming the City Maternity Hospital. The site is now occupied by St Martin's College.

The Lodge.   Flimby.

Flimby Lodge, a former ladies' school at Flimby, was purchased by the Cockermouth Union in 1886 for use as a school and vagrant wards. In 1914 there were thirty-one boys and fourteen girls in residence.

Wigton Hospital, though much altered and extended, still provides an attractive example of the '200-pauper' design often used by smaller or more rural unions. The original entrance block was at the right of the picture.

WHITEHAVEN

A workhouse was built on Scotch Street in Whitehaven in 1773. It was enlarged in 1795 to accommodate 200 inmates, following Whitehaven's adoption of Gilbert's Act. The parish of Preston Quarter had a workhouse at Ginns. In 1795, Harrington parish began to send its poor to the workhouse at Workington which Eden's State of the Poor described as 'a large and commodious Workhouse, which can take 150 persons. It is placed a little out of the town in an open, healthy situation, and was opened on the 28th October, 1793.'

After its formation in 1838, the Whitehaven Union used existing parish workhouse buildings at Whitehaven (for females) and at Preston Quarter (for males), each of which housed around 200.

In 1854-5, a new union workhouse was built on Low Road (now St Bees Road) at the south of Whitehaven (NX975163). It accommodated 424 inmates and cost £8,000. The workhouse also boasted 4 acres of gardens in which the inmates cultivated vegetables.

After 1930, the site was renamed Meadow View House and later became a geriatric hospital. Following subsidence caused by mine workings, the property was demolished in the early 1960s.

The old Workington workhouse, on what is now Ellerbeck Lane, was acquired in 1888 by the Workington Board of Health for use as a fever hospital. It was later part of Workington Infirmary but closed in 1965 and has been demolished. The administration building is now a private house. (CUW)

WIGTON

The Wigton Union initially made use of existing small workhouses at Caldbeck, Oulton, Glasson, and in Wigton itself at The Bog.

A new Wigton Union workhouse was built in 1838-42 on Cross Lane in Wigton (NY248490). The building had a very similar layout to the nearby Penrith and Cockermouth Union workhouses, all being based on the PLC's model '200-pauper plan'.

After 1930, the workhouse was renamed Highfield House Public Assistance Institution. Under the NHS it became Wigton Hospital which still occupies the site. (CUC)

CHAPTER 2

DURHAM

AUCKLAND

The first Auckland Union workhouse was a former parish workhouse on Newgate Street, Bishop Auckland. In 1855, a new union workhouse opened at the west side of Cockton Hill (NZ208290). Only eight years later, in 1863, overcrowding necessitated the building of an extension. A seventy-bed infirmary was added in 1877, together with casual wards, new board-room and offices. A further infirmary was added in 1909-11.

The workhouse later became Oaklands Poor Law Institution. In 1948, the site became Bishop Auckland General Hospital. Later redevelopment has resulted in the demolition of most of the former workhouse buildings. (DUR)

CHESTER-LE-STREET

The Chester-le-Street Union, formed in 1837, at first made use of existing workhouses at Chester-le-Street and Lambton. A new workhouse was eventually built in 1854-6 on Durham Road in Chester-le-Street (NZ274508).

The new workhouse originally comprised an entrance block at the east with central archway, a T-shaped main block some distance to the rear, and the workhouse infirmary behind.

In 1948, the former workhouse became a general hospital. More recently, as Chester-le-Street Hospital, it provided care for the elderly. Modern buildings now occupy the site. (DUR)

DARLINGTON

Darlington had a workhouse in Leadyard (NZ291144), on the banks of the River Skerne. The building, dating from around 1164 and previously an Episcopal palace, was purchased from the Bishop of Durham in 1806. In 1837, the building was taken over by the new Darlington Union and continued in use until a replacement workhouse was opened in 1870. The new building was erected on Yarm Road in Darlington (NZ301142) with accommodation for 250 inmates and fifty vagrants.

The new workhouse had a T-shaped main building. The long north end, facing the road, featured a tall central entrance archway with a tower above. Women's accommodation was at the west of the building and men's to the east. To the east of the main building was a long single-storey board-room building which also contained the porter's lodge, receiving ward, vagrants' wards, clothes-rooms, workshops, stone-breaking shed, coroner's and dissecting rooms, and hearse house. To the south of the workhouse was a two-storey U-shaped infirmary.

In the 1920s the site was known as Feetham Infirmary or New Feetham's Institute then, after 1930, as Darlington Municipal Institution. It later provided care for the elderly as East Haven Hospital. Virtually all the original workhouse buildings are now demolished. The former Guardians' Offices on East Street and Poplar Road were in use as Darlington Register Office until 1973. (DUR)

DURHAM

In the 1770s, local workhouses were in operation in the Durham city districts of St Giles (for up to twenty inmates), St Nicholas (fifty), Crossgate (eighteen), Elvet (twenty), and Framwellgate (twenty-four).

A new Durham Union workhouse was built in 1837 on Crossgate at the south-west of Durham (NZ269424). The architect was George Jackson. In 1857, the workhouse was described as a 'plain stone building, and contains ten rooms used as sleeping compartments, a dining-hall, which is also used as a chapel, a room for the use of the Board of Guardians, rooms for the sick, receiving wards, kitchens, pantry, and other requisite apartments; suitable school-rooms are also in the course of erection. The building is arranged to contain 125 inmates, besides a portion distinctly set apart for the separate use of vagrants.'

The casual ward block of the Auckland Union workhouse. During the First World War the workhouse provided beds for sick and wounded military personnel. In 1942, the hospital became the Bishop Auckland Emergency Hospital then from 1944 to 1947 it accommodated German prisoners of war.

The main building of the Chester-le-Street Union workhouse. In 1927, during a miners' dispute, the Chester-le-Street Guardians were suspended for making relief payments to unmarried miners, contrary to a ruling by the Ministry of Health. In their place, three new Guardians were appointed by the Ministry to run the union.

Over the years, Durham, like most unions, extended and updated its buildings. New casual wards were added at the east of the site in 1875, and a block for the infirm at around the same time. Here is the rather elegant new dining hall erected in 1891.

The workhouse later became Durham Poor Law Institution, then Crossgate Hospital, and after 1948, St Margaret's Hospital. Some of the surviving buildings have been converted to housing and others are used by local community organisations. (DUR)

EASINGTON

A workhouse was set up on Bishop Street in Easington in 1730.

The Easington Union, formed in 1837, appears to have operated without a workhouse until one was erected in 1850 on Seaside Lane at the north-east of Easington (NZ418435). The first Master and Matron of the workhouse were John and Mary Mason who, in 1851, had twenty-five inmates in their charge.

The buildings were gradually expanded taking the capacity to 130 in 1894. A hospital was erected at the east of the workhouse, and a nurses' home was added in 1926.

The former workhouse later became Leeholme Hospital but closed in 1971 and the buildings demolished. The Board of Guardians' offices from 1902 still survive. (DUR)

GATESHEAD

In the seventeenth century, Gateshead built a poor house in St Mary's churchyard. In 1750, another was acquired at the east of the High Street. The house, built as an almshouse under a bequest from Thomas Powell, was illegally converted to a poor house and then a workhouse, which it remained until 1841.

The Gateshead Union Guardians first met at the Goat Inn, Bottle Bank, on 14 December 1836. The union inherited five existing workhouses and it was at first decided to retain those at Gateshead and Heworth, and sell off the others at Swalwell, Winlaton and Ryton Woodside. However, in January 1838, it was decided that a new workhouse was required after all.

The site chosen was at Rector's Field (NZ250623), and the new workhouse for 276 inmates was ready in July 1841. Nearby residents of fashionable Claremount Place repeatedly complained about offensive smells from the workhouse but an investigation in 1848 revealed that these were caused by sewage from Claremount Place itself entering the workhouse grounds.

Frequent overcrowding at the workhouse led to bed-sharing and the slackening of the separation of children and adults. Expansion plans were hampered by the size of the existing site and in 1863 the Poor Law Board recommended a new workhouse be established elsewhere. However, the cost-conscious Guardians refused such a move and the overcrowding continued. By 1874, children were sleeping three to a bed. In the same year, there were two instances of girls in the workhouse having been made pregnant by inmates. By 1879, the workhouse had 550 inmates in residence.

In 1885, the Board acquired High Teams Farm at Bensham (NZ247612) on which to build a workhouse for 922 inmates, and a school for 300 children. The new workhouse opened in June 1890. It had four main areas: an entrance block with porter's lodge and casuals' and receiving wards on Workhouse Lane at the west; the main building with administrative offices, kitchens, and male and female wards; a hospital at the south-east of the site; and a school at the north.

After 1930, the site became High Teams Institution. In 1938, the medical facilities separated to become Bensham General Hospital. The remainder became Fountain View and later provided hostel accommodation for the homeless. Most of the old buildings were demolished in 1969.

Gateshead also a children's cottage homes site (NZ110534) and sanatorium (NZ103527) at Shotley Bridge. (TAW)

HARTLEPOOL

The Hartlepool Union was created in March 1859, from what had previously been the eastern part of the Sedgefield Poor Law Union. The new union erected a workhouse in 1860-1 on

Much of the preparatory work on the Gateshead High Teams site, such as levelling and brick-making, was done by unemployed men under a labour test scheme. Little now survives of the buildings except part of the original pavilion-plan infirmary. In recent times, as Bensham Hospital, the site has provided care for the elderly.

Holdforth Road at Throston (NZ500345). It was designed by Matthew Thompson, architect of the workhouses at Chester-le-Street and Houghton-le-Spring. The original building, at the south-east of the site, had a single-storey entrance block with entrance archway. A porter's lodge lay to the west of the entrance block, with casual wards behind. The main building was a two-storey red-brick building with a central dining-hall at its rear. The original workhouse infirmary stood behind.

A major expansion took place in 1889 with the erection of a 250-bed pavilion-plan hospital complex to the north of the workhouse, and a school for 500 children to the west.

The workhouse later became Howbeck Infirmary, then Hartlepool General Hospital, and is now the University Hospital of Hartlepool. Of late, only the lodge and parts of the 1889 hospital survived. (TSD)

HOUGHTON-LE-SPRING
In 1824, a township workhouse for around 200 inmates was erected at the east side of Sunderland Street in Houghton-le-Spring (NZ342501). Its governor in 1827 was John Snaith. In 1837, the building was taken over and adapted by the new Houghton-le-Spring Union.

A new workhouse was erected in 1864 at William Street in Houghton-le-Spring (NZ343500). It was designed by Matthew Thompson who was also the architect of workhouses for the Chester-le-Street, Hartlepool, and Weardale Unions. His design for Houghton-le-Spring had a corridor-plan T-shaped main block with male accommodation to the west and female to the east. Rooms for the aged were placed at the front of the building, and for children and able-bodied at the rear. A new board-room and offices were erected in 1891, with the old board-room then being converted into short-stay lunatic wards which included a padded room.

The former workhouse buildings no longer exist. (DUR)

LANCHESTER
A parliamentary report of 1777 recorded local workhouses in the Lanchester area at Tanfield and Kyo. Eden, in his 1797 survey of the poor in England, noted that Tanfield:

... contains about 2,000 inhabitants, mostly coal miners. Wages of labourers in husbandry are from 1s. 4d. to 1s. 6d. a day, and of coal miners, 2s. to 3s. Farms are small. Potatoes are much grown, which now form the chief diet of labourers' families. The cheapness of fuel seems the cause why this very useful vegetable is more used in the north than in the south of England. Here, as in other coal countries, the surface of the earth is neglected for the inside. There are about 20 Poor in the Workhouse.

The Lanchester Union workhouse was built in around 1839 on Newbiggin Road in Lanchester (NZ164475). The site expanded between 1880 and 1910 with additions including a hospital, union offices and cottage homes for children.

    After 1930, the establishment was renamed Lanchester Public Assistance Institution, then in about 1939 became Lee Hill Hospital until its closure and demolition in 1980. (DUR)

SEDGEFIELD

In 1663, Brian Harrison gave £100 for the poor of Sedgefield, of which £80 was used to purchase the workhouse and a cottage near Ryall.

    The first Sedgefield Union workhouse was an adaptation on an existing parish workhouse at the north of the town on the east side of King William Street, now East End (NZ359290). It could hold about fifty inmates.

    In 1860, a new Union workhouse was erected at the south of the town on West End (NZ353286). It was built of brick and could accommodate around ninety inmates. It appears to have had an entrance range with a central archway fronting onto the street at the north. At the centre was a T-shaped main block with further buildings such as the laundry and workshops to the rear. The workhouse was enlarged in 1913 with the addition of an infirmary block north-east of the main building. The workhouse buildings no longer exist and housing now stands on the site. (DUR)

SOUTH SHIELDS

In 1777, South Shields was recorded as having a workhouse with accommodation for fifty inmates. Eden's 1797 survey of the poor reported of South Shields that:

> There are 162 public houses in South Shields, but only one church, which was enlarged in 1786... The Poor are contracted for by a respectable person, at 2s. 6d. weekly, for provisions and clothes for each person maintained in the House of Industry, as it is called. The number of inmates is 73. Table of Diet: Breakfast–every day, hasty pudding; Dinner–Sunday and Wednesday, beef, etc.; Monday, Thursday, pease soup; Tuesday, Saturday, barley boiled in milk; Friday, suet dumplings. Supper–Sunday, Wednesday, broth and bread; Monday, Thursday, boiled milk; Tuesday, Saturday, bread and milk; Friday, cold milk.

In 1827, the South Shields workhouse was in West Holborn.

    The first South Shields Union workhouse was erected in 1837 on German Street – now Ocean Road (NZ369675). The architects were J. & B. Green whose design was based on the PLC's model '200-pauper' plan.

    By the 1870s, the German Street building was proving too small and it was decided to build a new workhouse at the edge of Harton Moor (NZ366643). It was designed by J.H. Morton and based on the popular pavilion-plan layout. The total cost including the purchase of 17 acres from the Church Commissioners was in the region of £55,000. The new workhouse opened in 1878, with space for 700 inmates.

Most of the Lanchester workhouse buildings have been demolished, but the entrance range and cottage homes survive (now used as housing), as do the union offices (now the local library).

After 1930, the workhouse became Harton Institution and General Hospital, then South Shields General Hospital in the late 1940s, and later South Tyneside District Hospital. Few of the original workhouse buildings now survive. (TAW)

STOCKTON-ON-TEES

A workhouse was set up on Bishop Street in Stockton in 1730. Corporation accounts for that year list a payment to a Mr Pewterer 'for his trouble of writing to the Bishop to obtain leave to dig his brick and build a Workhouse upon the waiste two dozen wine, which cost £2 6s 0d.'

In 1837, the new Stockton Union took over the existing Stockton workhouse, which could hold a maximum of forty inmates. The 1841 census records a total of thirty-two inmates, eighteen male and fourteen female, although the adult inmates were all female except for one man aged sixty. In May 1847, a report by Assistant Poor Law Commissioner H.J. Hawley noted that the workhouse was in use as a fever hospital following an outbreak of illness amongst the vagrants. In addition, there were no receiving wards, school, or separate sick-ward, and poor supervision of inmates.

In 1849-51, a new workhouse for 260 inmates was built at Portrack Lane, Stockton (NZ451196). The initial buildings occupied only half of the site. The main entrance block at the north fronted onto Portrack Road and contained the porter's lodge and Master's quarters. To its west were a receiving ward and the casual ward office. The main building had an E-shaped layout and contained male accommodation at the east and female at the west, with the dining hall in the central wing and a further ward block to the south. The original workhouse infirmary stood at the south-west of the main building but a large new block for male patients was erected in 1868 at the south-east of the site.

After 1930, the workhouse became Stockton Public Assistance Institution then in 1948 joined the NHS as Portrack Geriatric Hospital. In 1972 it was renamed St Anne's Hospital but closed a few years later and the buildings demolished. (DUR)

SUNDERLAND

Sunderland's first parish workhouse was built by public subscription in 1740 on Church Walk (later Trinity Place) near to the Parish Church. Trafalgar Square now covers what was the workhouse garden. At one time it housed over 600 inmates. Eden's 1797 survey of the poor reported of Sunderland that:

The South Shields workhouse comprised an entrance block, main building, infirmary and schools. By 1910, it was estimated that the cost to date had been £94,750 with the workhouse able to accommodate 1,200. Amongst the surviving buildings are the eastern pavilions of the workhouse, shown above.

Sunderland's 1855 workhouse was an unusual design constructed around two internal courtyards. It received it first occupants on 13 October 1855, when 306 inmates were transferred from the old Gill Bridge Avenue workhouse.

The main block of the Weardale Union workhouse at Stanhope, now converted to residential use after lying derelict for many years..

The Poor are supported partly in a Workhouse, partly at home. There are 176 persons at present in the house. There are 36 children, two-thirds of them bastards, who are employed in a pin factory. The boys are generally bound apprentices to the sea service. The remaining inmates are mostly old women and prostitutes. Few old men are found here, being mostly employed as scavengers, or picking oakum.

Monkwearmouth had a workhouse on Portobello Lane and another on Cage Hill which was pulled down after being gradually buried by ballast offloaded from ships in the vicinity.

There was a workhouse at Bishopwearmouth at the junction of Durham Road and Low Row, replaced in 1827 by a new and larger building to the south of what is now Gill Bridge Avenue (NZ394571). In 1829, 314 inmates worked at spinning, weaving and picking oakum.

After its formation in 1836, the new Sunderland Union purchased the Gill Bridge Avenue workhouse at Bishopwearmouth, which it altered and enlarged. In the early 1850s, pressure on workhouse accommodation greatly increased, partly due to an influx of Irish and Scots. In 1853, a Removal Officer was appointed to try and remove some of these back to their homelands.

In 1853-5, a new workhouse for up to 500 inmates was built at a site near Hylton Road (NZ380566). Large new hospital buildings were erected in 1867, followed by schools for 200 children. The hospital facilities were extended in the early 1900s, and children's cottage homes erected at the north of the site.

By 1930, the workhouse site was known as the Highfield Institute and Municipal Hospital, then after 1948, as Sunderland General Hospital. Many of the old workhouse blocks were demolished in the 1970s but a few parts survive. (TAW)

TEESDALE

A parliamentary report of 1777 recorded local workhouses in operation at Barnard Castle, Bowes, Egleston, Gainford and Middleton. In 1827, Barnard Castle's workhouse was recorded as being located on 'De Mains'. In the same year, a workhouse existed at Staindrop.

In 1838, a new Teesdale Union workhouse was erected at the east side of Galgate in Barnard Castle (NZ054169). The architect was John Green whose design was based on the PLC's model '200-pauper' workhouse plan.

The main workhouse buildings have been demolished but the infirmary and another block, possibly the infectious ward, still survive as office accommodation. (DUR)

WEARDALE

In 1777, a workhouse for up to sixty inmates was in operation at Wolsingham.

After its formation in 1837, the new Weardale Union took over an existing building at Stanhope (NY999391) as its workhouse. In 1851, the building could accommodate eighty inmates.

In 1866-7, the old workhouse was replaced by a new building on the same site, at the east side of Union Lane. The main building at the east of the site was a two-storey T-shaped block facing to the south-west. A single-storey dining-hall was attached at the centre rear. The workhouse infirmary stood on higher ground at the rear of the workhouse. An entrance block, originally two storeys but later reduced to one after a fire, stood at the west of the site. A casuals' ward was located to the west of the entrance and contained sleeping cells and stone-breaking cells. The stone-breaking cells originally had apertures, now blocked up, with grilles through which small pieces of broken stone were collected. A laundry block stood to the east of the casuals' ward.

The main building has now been converted for residential use. The entrance block, casuals' ward and laundry are now used by a residential care home. (DUR)

CHAPTER 3

LANCASHIRE

ASHTON-UNDER-LYNE

In 1729, a report from 'Ashton-under-Line' recorded that:

A workhouse is now erected here, and we felt an Advantage from it, even before it was finished; the Dread of what is called Confinement, having spurr'd on several of our Poor to labour for a Livelihood, which they would never have endeavoured, as long as they could have been relieved by the Parish-Rate, or by an Alms at our Doors; other Places are about to follow our Example.

The workhouse was located on Dungeon Street (now Market Street) in Ashton-under-Lyne (SJ940991), which, in 1837, was taken over and extended by the new Ashton-under-Lyne Union.

In 1849–50, a new workhouse for 500 inmates was built on a site at Chamber Hills to the north-east of the town, on what is now Fountain Street (SJ954995). Later additions included a new hospital block in 1866, a hospital block for females in 1873, and a large dining-hall, kitchens, steam laundries and washhouse in 1881. In 1906, a separately administered 288-bed pavilion-plan infirmary was erected at the north-east of the workhouse with a nurses' home alongside.

Later part of Tameside General Hospital, the main building was demolished in 2007.

BARROW-IN-FURNESS

Barrow-in-Furness was part of the Ulverston Union until April 1876 when it became a separately administered Poor Law Parish. Its paupers were temporarily accommodated in a building in Dalkeith Street until a new workhouse was built on the outskirts of the town at Roose (SD221689). The new workhouse opened in February 1880 and was the subject of an extensive report in the *Barrow Herald*, an extract of which is reproduced below.

The new Workhouse is erected on a fine and commanding site, eight acres in extent, near Roose Station. On entering the gateway to the right, are found two rooms for paupers' own clothing, with disinfecting rooms adjoining. Immediately adjoining these are receiving wards, in which paupers have to remain until they have been passed by the doctor. Leaving these outbuildings the workhouse is found on elevated ground on the left hand side. The building is on the pavilion system and consists of three blocks, the central block being for administrative purposes and the block to the right for female, and that to the left for male paupers. It may be urged that a building like this accommodating 350 paupers and erected at a cost of about £15,000, apart from the value of the land, is too large a scheme for Barrow with only 84 indoor paupers, but in providing this workhouse the promoters have looked well ahead and have put up a house to meet the requirements of the future. During the week the work of removing the paupers from the temporary workhouse to the new workhouse has been carried out satisfactorily, and the paupers are very comfortable in their new apartments, but they are almost lost in the immensity of space.

Because of its location, the workhouse was known locally as the 'Big House on the Hill'. During the First World War it served as a military hospital. After 1930, the former workhouse became Roose Institution, and then Roose Hospital. It later began to offer care for the mentally ill and, from 1939, provided a gynaecological service. The hospital closed in 1993 and was demolished a few years later.

In about 1905, the union erected a small group of children's cottage homes on Roose Road (SD214691). (CUB)

Ashton-under-Lyne's Fountain Street workhouse was constructed of stone from the nearby Barrack quarries. A later extension, at the left of the picture, unbalanced the original elegant symmetry of the main building.

BARTON-UPON-IRWELL

The townships of Barton-upon-Irwell, Flixton and Urmston originally formed part of the Chorlton Poor Law Union. In 1849 they joined with the townships of Clifton and Worsley to form a new Barton-upon-Irwell Union. Stretford joined shortly afterwards.

Prior to 1849, a workhouse accommodating 100 inmates had been in operation at Barton-upon-Irwell at Green Lane, Patricroft (SJ763985). In 1853, a new union workhouse accommodating 230 was established on the site, incorporating most of the existing buildings. An infirmary was added at the north of the site in 1879-80. In 1892-4, a major expansion and redevelopment took place.

The workhouse later became Green Lane Institution, then Bridgewater Hospital. The former workhouse blocks were later used for the care of psychiatric patients, while the infirmary building accommodated geriatric and infirm cases. The buildings were demolished in the 1990s and housing now stands on the site. (LAR)

BLACKBURN

In 1777, Blackburn had a workhouse for up to thirty inmates. The town erected a new workhouse in 1791 on Merchant Street (later Workhouse Lane, now Hutchinson Street), Grimshaw Park (SD683273).

The new Blackburn Union, formed in 1837, initially continued using the Merchant Street premises. Eventually, a new workhouse was opened in 1864 on Haslingden Road to the south-east of Blackburn (SD694268). It cost £30,000 to build, and accommodated 1,000 inmates.

In 1866, a Poor Law Board inspection found conditions there far from satisfactory:

> There is no effectual classification of cases; for example, in one ward is a poor woman suffering from cancer; she is reduced to a most distressing condition. Her disorder is so offensive that I

Barrow's cottage homes comprised an administrative building (right) and two pairs of semi-detached houses accommodating a total of seventy-seven children over the age of three. Each home had a foster mother to 'minister to their needs with such kindness and attention as they would receive in a good home'.

could not remain near her; yet several other patients occupy this ward with her and there are large and excellent wards in the workhouse which are unused. There is no proper supply of water in the water-closets, and these closets are so constructed that the foul air arising in them is drawn into the wards.

There are large wards near the entrance lodge which contain cases of 'venereal disease', and 'bad legs.' The porter and his wife are supposed to look after these cases, but they appear for the most part to be left to themselves. In the male ward were eight or ten men walking about almost naked. I was told 'they were getting their dinners.' The condition of the inmates of this ward was most distressing and painful to witness.

Better kind of beds is requisite for certain cases. In the women's lunatic ward I found one of the beds mildewed and decayed owing to neglect. Some of the able-bodied men sleep together two in each bed – a most objectionable custom.

There are great dissensions amongst the officers of this workhouse, and the management is therefore lax and disorganised. Almost all the male officers have brought charges against each other, chiefly of absence from duty, and drunkenness.

The master especially is charged with intoxication. Although the master knew I was in the workhouse he did not appear. I sent repeatedly for him, and the reply was, in each instance, that he could not be found. Under such circumstances I cannot but suspect that he was not sober enough to come before me.

Not surprisingly, the Master was removed from his office shortly after this report was made.

After 1929, the establishment came under the control of the County Borough of Blackburn and was known as the Queen's Park Institution. In more recent times, as Queens Park Hospital, the site has provided a variety of medical care services for the area. (LAR)

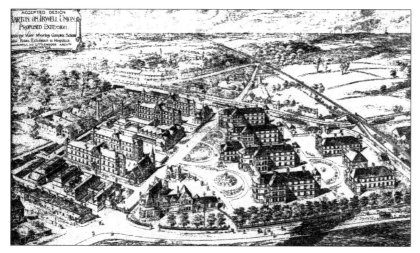

In 1891, the design for the expansion of Barton-upon-Irwell workhouse was opened to competition. The winning scheme by Magnall and Littlewood of Manchester featured a large pavilion-plan hospital. Only a much reduced version of the scheme was actually built, however.

Blackburn Union workhouse – its prominent and elevated location was said to have been chosen as a constant reminder of its presence to the local population. However, by 1920, attitudes had clearly softened when a patients' cinema was installed at the workhouse.

BOLTON

Like many other northern unions, Bolton declined to build a new central union workhouse. From 1837, it continued using existing small workhouses on Fletcher Street in Bolton (SD714083) and at Goose Cote Farm, Turton (SD719144).

In 1858, following pressure from the Poor Law Board to erect a new workhouse, the Guardians acquired a site known as Fishpool Farm at Farnworth (SD718064). Construction of new buildings for up to 1,045 inmates cost around £25,000. The institution was opened by then Chairman of the Guardians, Dan Wood Lantham, on 26 September 1861.

Built in the then fashionable Italianate style, the main building was dominated by a 72-foot high tower which concealed a large water tank at its top. The northern side of the main building housed male inmates, while females were in the southern side.

In the mid-1870s, Bolton was one of the first unions to adopt the cottage homes system for its children. Situated to the south of the workhouse, the site (later known as Hollins Cottage Homes) eventually included ten cottages, a school, gymnasium, stores and superintendent's house.

In 1894, a further 76 acres of land were purchased at the north of the workhouse, and a new pavilion-plan infirmary, which became known as Townley's Hospital, was erected.

After 1930, the workhouse was renamed Fishpool Public Assistance Institution. The site subsequently became the Bolton District General Hospital, now the Royal Bolton Hospital. (BOL)

BURNLEY

In 1837, the new Burnley Poor Law Union took over old workhouse buildings on Royle Road in Burnley (SD838329) and on the Blackburn Road at Padiham (SD780333), which between them provided over 300 places.

A new workhouse for 500 inmates was eventually erected on Briercliffe Road in Burnley (SD851347), admitting its first inmates in March 1876. The buildings, designed by William Waddington of Burnley, cost about £20,000. The buildings were constructed in the then popular Italianate style with stone from the Tubber Hill and Burnley Lane quarries. The main building was three storeys high with a T-shaped layout. Administrative functions were located at the centre, with males placed in the west wing, and women in the east. There were dayrooms on the ground floor, for the aged and imbeciles at the front, and for able-bodied and children at the rear. A corridor ran the length of each wing with iron gates between each section. A large pavilion-plan infirmary was added in 1895 to the north of the existing infirmary.

After 1930, control of the workhouse passed to Burnley Public Assistance Committee. The infirmary was taken over by the separate Public Health Committee and was renamed Primrose Bank Hospital. Following the inauguration of the NHS in 1948, the two parts were reunited and became Burnley General Hospital. The buildings were demolished in 2008. (LAN)

BURY

Prior to 1834, township workhouses operated on Manchester Road at Bury (SD804088), on Blackburn Street at Radcliffe (SD783073), on Bury Old Road at Heap, on Moss Lane at Pilkington (SD812061), and at Tottington Lower End (SD780152).

The Bury Union, formed in 1837, continued using several of the old township workhouses. However, in 1850, Lord Derby, refused to renew leases for the Bury, Heap and Pilkington workhouses which stood on his land, saying that the Guardians had 'already spent as much money as would have built a union workhouse by paying extra salaries and not having a labour test.'

In 1851, the Poor Law Board proposed that Bury and the adjacent Rochdale union build a joint workhouse. However, Bury decided to go it alone and, in 1852, the Guardians borrowed £6,000 and advertised for plans for a workhouse for 400 inmates, with a separate sixty-bed hospital. Work on the new buildings began in 1855 at Jericho (SD832116). By 1857, the total cost had swollen to £20,481.

In 1876, a new thirty-two-bed infectious hospital was built with four ward-blocks connected by a wide, open covered way. A report at the time described the wards as 'excellent in themselves and greatly in advance of anything hitherto attempted'. In 1905, a new 126-bed pavilion-plan infirmary opened at the south of the workhouse. In 1914, a wartime military hospital was established at the site.

The workhouse later became Bury Union Institution, then Jericho Institution. In 1940, it was used as a decontamination centre. In the same year, a bomb fell in the grounds but caused relatively little damage or injury.

The site is now known as Fairfield Hospital and most of the old workhouse blocks have been replaced by modern buildings. (BRY, MAN)

The Italianate grandeur of Bolton's main building – a style very much in vogue in the mid-nineteenth century and characterised by a gently pitched roof, overhanging eaves, pinnacles, and round-topped sash windows often grouped in threes.

Burnley workhouse's main building with a 70-foot-high tower at its centre. On the ground floor were the Guardians' board-room, master's offices, and a store for inmates' own clothes. The Master's and Matron's bedrooms were on the first floor above.

Caton, Lancashire's only Gilbert Union workhouse, was declared 'wholly unsuitable for the reception, and proper care and management of the poor' after a Poor Law Board inspection in 1866.

A 1906 view of Chorley workhouse – described in an 1887 directory as 'a handsome structure in Victorian style'.

CATON GILBERT UNION

In 1822, Caton and seven other parishes and townships formed a Gilbert Union. A further thirteen parishes joined in 1829. The union erected a workhouse to the south-east of Caton (SD546639).

Its Gilbert Union status exempted Caton from most of the provisions of the 1834 Poor Law Amendment Act. An inspection of the premises by the Poor Law Board in 1866 resulted in a catalogue of criticisms. There were no receiving wards, vagrant wards, insane wards, infirmary or school. There was no water-closet, bath or lavatory, and the men slept two to a bed. Two men who were confined to their beds were in the charge of another pauper who was so deaf they could not make him hear. An insane woman temporarily placed in the workhouse had thrown herself from a window and was killed. Another lunatic inmate had cut his own throat with a razor.

Despite ongoing efforts by the PLC to persuade the union to dissolve itself, it survived until 1869 when all remaining Gilbert Unions were abolished. A new Lunesdale Poor Law Union was formed which took in most of the Caton Union's former members. (LAN)

CHORLEY

In 1837, the new Chorley Union took over existing local workhouses at Eaves Lane in Chorley (SD592178), Brindle (SD594230), Croston (SD492189) and Leyland (SD541227). By the 1860s, Croston and Leyland had closed, with the majority of the union's paupers then being housed at Brindle, and Eaves Lane used for the temporary accommodation of invalids and vagrants.

A Poor Law Inspector's report in 1866 described Brindle as 'a ruinous old place… quite unfit for the purpose for which it used' and Eaves Lane as 'very old and ill-arranged'. The Guardians resolved to put their house in order and in 1870-2 a new workhouse for 320 inmates was erected on the Eaves Lane site at a cost of £25,000. Designed by T.T. Bradshaw, it comprised a porter's lodge and vagrants' accommodation at the site entrance to the north, a large T-shaped main block, and male and female hospital pavilions to the rear.

The workhouse later became Eaves Lane Hospital providing mental health care. The site is now occupied by housing. (LAN)

CHORLTON

The first Chorlton Union workhouse was at the junction of Stretford New Road and Leaf Street and accommodated 300 inmates. It soon proved inadequate to cope with the demands of the rapidly increasing population of the area. However, the site was not capable of being expanded, so a new workhouse was built on a greenfield site at Barlow Moor, Withington (SJ836924), at the north side of what is now Nell Lane. The building, erected in 1854-5, cost about £53,000 and accommodated up to 1,500 inmates.

In 1864-6 a pavilion-plan hospital, the first of its type in England, was erected at the north of the workhouse. Designed by Thomas Worthington, it comprised five well-spaced ward blocks, linked by a covered way, and each accommodating ninety-six patients. Worthington's design was praised by Florence Nightingale: 'Your hospital plan is a very good one: when completed it will be one of the best, if not the best, in the country.'

An account of a visit to the workhouse in 1881 included the following encounter:

We then entered the old women's sitting-room, where the dear old creatures past all work sit and croon and twiddle their thumbs. It is true some of them make a pretence of doing a little darning, but they seem quite at liberty to do as much or as little as they like. One very sprightly old woman of over eighty appears to be a sort of chartered grumbler, and we were informed by the Governor that she always succeeded in getting in the last word. Strange as the occupation may seem for a woman she had formerly been a sweep, and she told us with pardonable pride that she had been up many a chimney, petticoats and all. Her name is Becky Mathews, and each remark she makes comes out with a report like a fog signal. When asked if the soup was better today she said, 'No'. When reminded that fewer peas had been put in to please her, she jerked out, 'It's not to please me, it's to save the peas.'

In 1880, the union erected a new children's home and school opposite the workhouse at the south of Nell Lane. In 1898, the children were transferred to new cottage homes at Styal (SJ844828). The old schools were then adapted for use as additional hospital accommodation.

In 1915, the workhouse was transferred to the Manchester Union Guardians and renamed Withington Hospital. Most of the hospital closed in 2002 and much of the site has since been redeveloped. (MAN)

CLITHEROE

A parliamentary report of 1777 recorded a township workhouse in operation at Bolton by Bowland accommodating up to ten inmates. A workhouse was erected near Aighton in 1817.

For many years, Clitheroe Union resisted the building of a new workhouse and made use of the existing workhouses at Aighton (SD694399) and Bolton-by-Bowland (SD774496). These old buildings were severely criticised by an 1866 official inspection which found that Holden was 'old, irregular and dilapidated'. Aighton was so remote that the Guardians' Visiting Committee inspected the workhouse once a year rather than the more usual once a fortnight. The Guardians' own board-room was little better however. Situated above some stables and cowsheds, it was described by the inspector as the most incommodious and uncomfortable he had ever visited. The waiting-room for relief applicants was a cellar accessed by some 'ruinous' stone steps which became awash with water in wet weather.

An aerial view of Chorlton's Withington site with the workhouse main building left of centre and Thomas Worthington's influential pavilion-plan infirmary to its rear. The large cultivated areas in the foreground provided both work for the inmates and produce for their consumption.

In 1915, Chorlton and Prestwich joined Manchester township to form a new Manchester Union, with the Chorlton workhouse becoming Withington Hospital. This view of the entrance from around that date shows the former workhouse chapel at the centre.

Chorlton's cottage homes at Styal were home to up to 500 pauper children. As well as the cottages, each of which contained up to twenty beds, the site included a school, workshops, laundry, stores, a swimming bath, hospital and a probationers' lodge where newcomers were quarantined for a fortnight. The site is now occupied by Styal women's prison.

Styal Cottage Homes Entrance.

The main building of the former Clitheroe Union workhouse – now part of Clitheroe Community Hospital.

Following this report, the Guardians agreed to replace the old buildings. A new workhouse, for 200 inmates, together with a thirty-six-bed hospital, was erected in 1870-73 at the south side of Chatburn Road in Clitheroe (SD755430).

After 1930, the site became Coplow View Public Assistance Infirmary, then joined the NHS as Clitheroe Hospital – now Clitheroe Community Hospital. (LAN)

FYLDE

Kirkham had a workhouse from around 1726 on Back Lane, now Marsden Street (SD424320). In 1837, the Kirkham site was taken over by the new Fylde Union, despite the petitions of Poulton-le-Fylde, the only other settlement in the Fylde to have a workhouse.

In 1844, a new union workhouse was opened on Moor Lane in Kirkham (SD422321). It broadly followed the popular 'square' layout with the different classes of inmate accommodated in separate wings radiating from a central hub.

In 1907, the union opened a new and larger workhouse at Wesham. The old Kirkham building was used for a few years as a children's home, then in 1913 was replaced by a group of children's cottage homes on the same site.

The new Wesham workhouse (SD420329), designed by Charles S. Haywood and Fred Harrison, used the then popular pavilion plan. There were separate blocks for the able-bodied and aged inmates of both sexes, for mothers and infants, and for infirm females, and also two-roomed 'cottages' for married couples. All these linked by a wide, covered corridor to a central administrative block. At the rear of the site were a laundry, bakery, boiler house and a 100-bed infirmary. The porter's office, receiving-rooms, and a vagrants' block for twenty-five tramps lay at the entrance to the site. A separate block contained offices and board-room. Water for the workhouse was pumped from underground and stored in a large water tower.

The site later became Wesham Park Hospital. This has now closed although some surviving buildings have latterly been used as NHS Trust office accommodation. (LAN)

GARSTANG

The Garstang Poor Law Union was formed in January 1837 and took over an existing workhouse operated building at Claughton (SD505427) dating from 1795.

In 1866, a Poor Law Board Inspector found that the building was 'extremely defective'. Amongst the numerous faults was a complete absence of water-closets, lavatories or baths. Anyone wanting to wash had to 'go down to the brook' that bounded one part of the premises. A highly offensive-smelling bedroom was said to be occupied by three men with 'bad legs'.

In 1876, a new workhouse accommodating sixty-seven inmates was built at Bowgreave (SD497444). It comprised an entrance lodge, casuals' ward and a T-shaped main block.

The Bowgreave workhouse buildings no longer exist. (LAN)

HASLINGDEN

Haslingden had a town workhouse for up to 150 inmates on Spring Lane (SD786237) dating from 1749. The site was later occupied by the Haslingden Brewery. There was also a workhouse for up to 200 inmates at Newchurch (SD854223).

Like many northern unions, Haslingden was unenthusiastic about the New Poor Law. Attendance at early Guardians' meetings was desultory – between June 1838 and June 1839, an average of four of the total eighteen Guardians were present. However, attendances were often higher for meetings held at the Commercial Inn rather than the Haslingden National School!

Initially, the union rented the existing workhouses at Spring Lane and Newchurch. The administration of these establishments fell considerably short of official requirements: classification and segregation were poor, and inmates wore their own clothes and were allowed to smoke. New arrivals at Haslingden workhouse were first placed in the kitchen before being taken to the wash-house and washed in a tub. From 1851, Haslingden workhouse was used only for male inmates while females were sent to Newchurch.

In 1864, the Haslingden Guardians asked the Lancashire & Yorkshire Railway for permission to place collecting boxes at local railway stations, so that travellers could donate discarded books and periodicals. The Guardians appear to have been surprised when told that one was full – in 1872. One box was still in use at Bacup station in 1919.

A rise in inmate numbers, together with continuing pressure from the Poor Law Board, led to the erection in 1868-9 of a new union workhouse at Higher Pikelaw (SD797225), midway between Haslingden and Rawtenstall. Designed by Lockwood & Mawson, it had an impressive three-storey main building, and a separate eighty-eight-bed infirmary. The new workhouse opened in February 1870 with inmates from the old Haslingden workhouse being led to the new building by 'Blind Tom' Barnes playing 'See the Conquering Hero Comes' on his flute.

A major expansion of the site to the north-east of the workhouse began in 1912 with the opening of a new infirmary to the north-east of the workhouse.

The workhouse later became Moorland House Public Assistance Institution, and then Rossendale General Hospital which closed in 2010. (MAN)

LANCASTER

Lancaster built a workhouse on the south side of Quernmore Road (SD486614) in 1788. Eden's 1797 survey of the poor in England reported of Lancaster's workhouse that:

…there are 57 inmates, mostly old women and children. They are employed in picking cotton, one woman spins silk, and one labourer goes out to work. He gets 12s. a week, more than is earned by all the other paupers in the house. The Workhouse, which was built a few years ago, stands on an elevated healthy situation on the common. In each room there are 2 beds, partly filled with chaff, and partly with straw. Neatness and regularity are much attended to. Four cows are generally kept, from which near £20 are annually made by the sale of butter, none of which

A rare view of the Fylde Union's first workhouse two years before its closure in 1907. The buildings were demolished in 1912 to make way for children's cottage homes.

A view from about 1915 of the Fylde Union's new cottage homes which consisted of three houses on Moor Street and a superintendent's house on Station Road. The former cottage homes are now occupied by a medical centre and social services offices.

An early view of Fylde's Wesham workhouse. At the left is the board-room block, while in the distance are the female and infirm ward blocks. The water-tower acted as a reservoir for water drawn from a well in the grounds.

An early 1900s view of Haslingden's imposing union workhouse. Located at Higher Pikelaw on the west side of the Rossendale valley, midway between Haslingden and Rawtenstall, it stood a lofty 900 feet above sea level.

is used in the house, except for the sick and the governor and governess... Oatcake leavened is the common bread in Lancashire. It is preferred to any other.

The new Lancaster Union took over the existing Quernmore Road premises and greatly enlarged them in 1840-41 at a cost of £4,000. Later additions included a new porter's lodge and receiving wards at the north of the site in 1889, an infectious hospital, and a children's home.

After 1930, the workhouse became Parkside Institution under the control of Lancashire County Council Public Assistance Committee.

The main workhouse building no longer exists. The surviving structures now form part of the Lancaster Royal Grammar School premises. (LAN)

LEIGH

A building on King Street in Leigh served as a workhouse from 1750 to 1823. Early workhouses also operated at Culcheth, Tyldesley and Lowton.

In its early years, the Leigh Union continued to use existing local workhouses at Culcheth (SJ655952) and Lowton (SJ614966). A new union workhouse was erected on a site at the east side of Leigh Road (SD658013) in 1850-1 at a cost of £8,000. It was later described as a 'fine gothic building' and accommodated 400 inmates.

In 1885, a 122-bed infirmary was added at a cost of £11,000. In 1896, a further £12,000 was spent on new offices, a steam laundry, workshops, stables and new vagrant wards. In 1907-8, a new men's pavilion was added, followed by a similar one for women in 1913, taking the capacity to 500.

Under the NHS, the site became Atherleigh Hospital. Since its closure in 1990, the buildings have been demolished and replaced by modern housing. (WIG)

The entrance to the Lancaster Union workhouse where new arrivals would present themselves, and where vagrants would queue up for the 5 p.m. opening of the casual ward.

LIVERPOOL

In 1732, Liverpool erected a workhouse at the corner of College Lane and Hanover Street. A new 'House of Industry' for 600 inmates was built in 1769-72 at Brownlow Hill (SJ357902). In 1797, Eden reported that 1,220 people were in the workhouse:

> The old people in particular are provided with lodging in a most judicious manner. Each apartment consists of three small rooms, in which are the fire-place and 4 beds, and is inhabited by 8 or 10 persons. These habitations are furnished with beds, chairs, and other little articles of domestic use that the inmates may possess, who being thus detached from the rest of the Poor, may consider themselves as comfortably lodged as in a secluded cottage, and thus enjoy, even in a Workhouse, in some degree, the comfort of a private fireside. The most infirm live on the ground floor; others are distributed through the upper storeys. They all dine together in a large room, which occasionally serves as a chapel. The children are mostly employed in picking cotton, but are too crowded, 70 or 80 working in a small room. About 50 girls are bound apprentices in sprigging muslin. About 2,700 out pensioners are also relieved, at a weekly expense of £56 9s. The committee refuse relief to such Poor as keep dogs.

In 1823, three remarkably long-lived workhouse residents died: Ellen Tate aged 110, Francis Dixon aged 105, and Margaret McKenzie aged 104.

Liverpool resisted the implementation of the 1834 Act but, on 25 March, 1841, it was constituted as a single Poor Law Parish – its population (in 1831) of 165,175 making it the largest in England. However, within a year, continued petitioning led to the passing of a Local Act allowing the parish to revert to its former management by a Select Vestry.

Liverpool continued to use the Brownlow Hill workhouse which was enlarged in 1842-3 with

Leigh Union workhouse, described by an 1873 directory as a 'fine Gothic building' The palatial-looking new Guardians' offices are at the right of centre.

Lockwood & Allom as architects. It became one of the largest workhouses in the country with an official capacity of over 3,000 inmates, and accommodating as many as 5,000 on occasion.

On 7 September 1862, a serious fire at the workhouse destroyed the church and one of the children's dormitories. Twenty-one children and two nurses were burnt to death.

In 1865, Liverpool pioneered the use of trained nurses in workhouses when local philanthropist William Rathbone funded the placement in the workhouse infirmary of twelve nurses trained at London's Nightingale School. These were assisted by eighteen probationers and fifty-four able-bodied female inmates who received a small salary. Although the experiment had mixed results – the pauper assistants needed constant supervision and obtained intoxicants at the slightest opportunity – it was generally perceived as a success, in large part due to the efforts of the infirmary superintendent, Agnes Jones. Eventually a skilled nursing system spread to all union infirmaries in the country.

The workhouse was demolished in 1931 to make way for the new Roman Catholic cathedral.

Liverpool also erected an Industrial School in 1843-5 at Bootle Lane, Kirkdale (SJ350941), and cottage homes in 1899 at Olive Mount, Wavertree (SJ395898). (LIV)

LUNESDALE

The Lunesdale Poor Law Union was created in 1869 following the abolition of the Caton Gilbert Union, many of whose member parishes it inherited.

The new Lunesdale Union workhouse was erected in 1872 at a site to the south of Hornby (SD584677). It had a simple T-shaped main building facing to the north. The entrance and Master's quarters were at the centre, with separate male and female accommodation to each side. A separate block to the south may have been a small infirmary.

The buildings were later used as offices but have now been converted to residential use. (LAN)

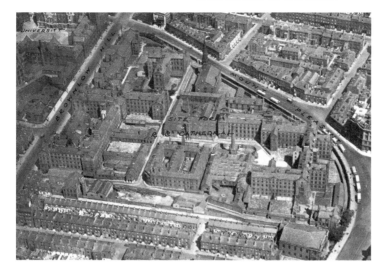

An aerial view of Britain's biggest workhouse set between Brownlow Hill (left) and Mount Pleasant (diagonal) in Liverpool. The site was cleared soon afterwards to make way for Sir Edwyn Lutyens' Roman Catholic Cathedral.

The Mount Pleasant entrance of the Liverpool Workhouse in about 1925.

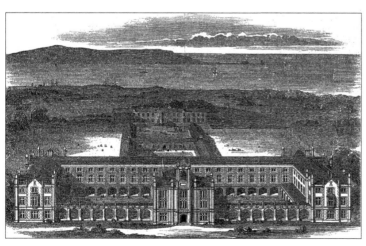

Kirkdale School was 'one of the principal architectural ornaments of the vicinity of Liverpool'. Its 1,150 children were instructed 'not only in the elements of a plain education – reading, writing, and arithmetic – and in their religious duties, but in the most common and useful trades.' It later became Kirkdale Homes for the aged and infirm, then Westminster House Home, before finally closing in March 1968.

Liverpool's Wavertree Cottage Homes opened in 1899 and included sixteen children's cottages homes, two schools and a superintendent's house. Most of the buildings were demolished in 1993.

MANCHESTER

A parliamentary survey in 1777 recorded a workhouse in Manchester for up to 180 inmates. Workhouses were also in use at Cheetham, Failsworth, Harpurhey and Great Heaton.

A workhouse was built in 1792 on New Bridge Street in Manchester. In 1797, Eden reported that there were 319 persons in residence, mainly old women and children, who were mostly employed in winding yarn. However, further details were unobtainable as 'a malignant fever now rages with great violence in the house, and renders it unsafe to enter it.' Breaking workhouse rules was punished 'by confinement in the stocks, or in the dungeon, or elsewhere, or by distinction of dress, by abatement of diet, loss of gratuity, by such corporal or other punishment as may be determined... by the Weekly Board of Overseers.'

A Manchester Poor Law Union was created in December 1840, and continued to use the Bridge Street workhouse (SJ835983) and one on Moston Lane at Harpurhey (SD866019).

In 1843, the union erected a large industrial school at Swinton (SD775016) at a cost of £60,000.

Rapid population growth in the 1840s led, in 1850, to Manchester becoming a Poor Law Parish in its own right. The other Manchester parishes formed a new Prestwich Union.

A new Manchester Parish workhouse was built in 1855-6 at Crumpsall (SD849022). Designed by Mills & Murgatroyd, it could house 1,660 inmates. The aged and infirm remained at New Bridge Street until 1875 when most of the site was sold to make way for an extension to Victoria station. The following year, a large new infirmary was erected at Crumpsall, to the north of the workhouse.

In 1915, Poor Law Unions in the Manchester area were reorganised, with the Manchester and Prestwich Unions amalgamating under the control of the Manchester Board of Guardians. The Crumpsall site was renamed the Crescent Road Institution.

The former Lunesdale workhouse – the segments for different classes of inmate have now became individual houses.

In 1930, the Manchester workhouse was taken over by the Manchester Public Assistance Committee, while the infirmary came under its Hospitals sub-committee. Under the name of Crumpsall Institution, the former workhouse became a centre for treatment of the mentally ill. It was renamed Park House in 1939, then in 1948 became Springfield Hospital. The site is now the North Manchester General Hospital. (MAN)

OLDHAM

Oldham's first workhouse was built in around 1730 at Side o'th' Moor (SD937051) at the junction of the present Lees Road and Glodwick Road.

There were also workhouses in Royton at the top of Mill Lane in Haggate (SD912076), in Chadderton near the present Stockfield Road (SD911050) and at Middleton on Hollin Lane (SD865077) which served both Middleton and Thornham. Small establishments operated at Crompton on Oldham Road in Shaw Side (SD937084) and at Tonge.

Oldham was particularly resistant to the 1834 Act, which it argued was inappropriate for the needs of a manufacturing area. It was ten years after the union's formation when the Oldham Board of Guardians finally met for the first time on 22 September 1847, at Oldham Town Hall. They reviewed the existing workhouses within their jurisdiction and decided that none was suitable for continued use, with those at Crompton and Tonge being particularly bad. Those at Oldham, Middleton, Royton and Chadderton were kept open until new accommodation could be provided.

Construction of a new workhouse began in 1848 on a site at Northmoor (SD920062). Designed by Manchester architects Travis & Magnall, it was completed in 1851 at a cost of £13,305.

The administration block of Manchester's Crumpsall workhouse – the Guardians' board-room was located on the first floor. The workhouse could accommodate 1,660 comprising: 745 able-bodied men and women; 152 women including 76 with infants; 248 idiots, imbeciles and epileptics; 255 children under sixteen; 60 probationers; and 200 sick.

In 1894, having received instruction from Inspector Harrison of the Oldham Corporation Fire Brigade, a number of the staff combined to form the Workhouse Fire Brigade.

In 1915, the workhouse was renamed Westwood Park Poor Law Institution. In the 1940s, the former workhouse hospital buildings on Sheepfoot Lane became Boundary Park General Hospital, with the rest of the buildings as an annexe providing geriatric and psychiatric care. The old buildings continued in use for many years as part of what became Oldham and District General Hospital. In 1981, major reconstruction of the hospital began, and on 1 December 1989, the Royal Oldham Hospital opened on the site of the old workhouse.

Oldham Union also had a children's home at Royton (SD917086). (OLD)

ORMSKIRK

In 1777, local workhouses were in operation in Ormskirk (for up to 114 inmates), Aughton (114 inmates), and Melling with Cunscough (fifty inmates). Ormskirk's workhouse was on Moor Street (SD416081) at the east side of the junction with what is now St Helen's Road.

After its formation in 1837, the Ormskirk Union took over the Moor Street workhouse. A new union workhouse was erected in 1851-3 at the south side of the Wigan Road in Ormskirk (SD421081). It was designed by William Culshaw who was also the architect of much larger workhouses for the Toxteth Park and West Derby Unions. His design for Ormskirk harked back to the cruciform layout popular during the peak workhouse building period of 1835-8. A two-storey entrance block stood facing the road at the north, and at the rear, four wings radiated from a central octagonal hub. In 1898, new union offices were erected to the east of the workhouse.

The site later became the Ormskirk and District General Hospital. Some original buildings still survive. (LAN)

PRESCOT

Prescot's first workhouse dated from 1707 and was founded by Oliver Lyme in rented almshouses on the Prescot to Rainhill Road. In 1777, parish workhouses were recorded in operation at Prescott (for up to eighty inmates), Ditton (fifty), Eccleston (fifty), Hale (fifty), Halewood (forty), Rainford (fifteen), Speak (fifty), Sutton (thirty) and Widnes (fifty). Sutton operated a workhouse at Marshall's Cross in St Helen's, and Windle had one on Ormskirk Street, also in St Helen's. Much Woolton and Whiston also ran local workhouses.

Prescot Poor Law union was formed in January 1837. Opposition to the new regime briefly surfaced in St Helen's with the Revd James Furnival attacking its 'vigour and cruelty'. By 1839, Furnival had clearly had a change of heart, accepting a £50 salary to become the Union's chaplain.

Initially, the union adopted the existing building at Windle (SJ511955) for its main workhouse, with the elderly being placed at Marshall's Cross workhouse (SJ523926, now the site of Sherdley primary school), and children at Much Woolton.

In 1842-3 a new Prescot Union workhouse was built on the Warrington Road at Whiston (SJ478919). Its layout used the popular cruciform design with an entrance block facing the road at the north. To the rear, four accommodation wings radiated from the central octagonal hub. In 1876, a T-shaped school block was added to the south wing, and a chapel was erected in 1881.

The former Prescot workhouse, now demolished, later became Whiston Hospital. (LAN)

PRESTON

Preston erected a workhouse in 1788 at the west side of Deepdale Road (SD544303). Other township workhouses in the area included Penwortham (SD532276, erected 1796), Walton-le-Dale (SD565260, 1796), Longton (1821), Ribchester (SD627366, 1823), Wood Plumpton (SD499357, 1824), Howick (1827) and Hutton (SD519260, 1827).

In 1829, the 'House of Recovery', a fever hospital, opened to the south of the workhouse (SD544302) – the institution was originally established in 1813 on a site near Trinity Church.

Like many parts of the industrial north, Preston opposed the 1834 Poor Law Act, preferring to distribute out-relief in times of industrial slump. In 1837, after reviewing the workhouses it had inherited, the new Preston Union closed and sold off the Howick, Hutton and Longton workhouses. Deepdale Road and Wood Plumpton stayed as mixed workhouses, Ribchester was used for adult males, Walton-le-Dale became the union's boys' school, and Penwortham was used for girls. The Preston House of Recovery became the union's fever hospital.

By the 1860s, Deepdale Road could accommodate 480 adults. Conditions there were severely criticised by an official inspection in November 1866:

> This workhouse is old, ill arranged, and unsuitable in every respect for the purposes for which it is used, namely, the reception of all classes of poor. The wards are for the most part dark, low, close, gloomy, and unhealthy; they are dangerously crowded with inmates, especially in the infirm and sick wards. Many of the infirm people, men as well as women, are sleeping together two in a bed. The sick have not all of them a separate bed to lie upon. In the 'venereal ward' the patients affected with syphilis are sleeping together two in a bed. Two women, owing to a want of room, have lately been placed together in the same bed in the lying-in ward, both having just been confined. Four patients, two men and two boys, were lately sleeping together in the same bed in the 'itch ward'. Six men occupied two beds in this ward to-day, three in each bed. The man lying in the middle of the bed had his feet to the top of the bed, and his head came out at the bottom of it. The feet of the other two men were placed so as to be close to the head of the man who was lying between them. In the midst of this ward, and in full view of the others, boys and men, an adult patient was

A 1930s view of the former Oldham workhouse – a typical example of the evolution from poor law institution into hospital.

The distinctive central hub illustrates this building's origins as the former Ormskirk workhouse, now part of Ormskirk and District General Hospital.

The long, low-rise profile of the Prescot workhouse which later became Whiston Hospital.

standing upright without a fragment of clothes upon him, whilst a pauper attendant painted him over with a brush dipped in an application for his disease.

However, a large new union workhouse was already in the progress of being erected on Watling Street Road in Fulwood (SD540317). Intended to accommodate up to 1,500 inmates, it was originally planned to cost £30,000. However, the final total was in the region of £50,000 and by 1870 the crippling loan charges against the project stood at £87,761.

The workhouse later became known as Preston Civic Hostel and more recently was used by a local college and business centre. The infirmary became Sharoe Green Hospital, dealing with geriatric cases, but has now been demolished as part of a redevelopment of the whole site.

The workhouse at Ribchester was adapted in 1856 to include special accommodation for lunatics and imbeciles. It later became Ribchester Hospital but has now closed. (LAN)

PRESTWICH

Prestwich Union was formed in 1850, mostly from districts previously part of the Manchester Union whose growing population had necessitated the reorganisation. Initially, Prestwich made use of an old workhouse on Rainsough Brow (SD809022) erected in 1819 to hold 120 paupers.

The old workhouse did not fare well in official inspections, which criticised its poor classification, overcrowded sick wards, and lack of a paid nurse. An 1866 inspection found that:

A pauper inmate attends upon the patients in each ward, neither of them can read writing. The 'woman' is told by the porter how to give the medicines, &c. The man states that there is generally a patient in the ward who can read, and he asks him what are the directions on the bottles, &c. Of course there is no security that the right medicine is given to the right patient, or that it is given at the proper time and in the correct quantities.

A new workhouse for 312 inmates was built in 1869-71 at Crumpsall (SD849025) to the north of Manchester, adjacent to the Manchester Township workhouse. It was designed by Thomas Worthington, architect of Chorlton Union infirmary. The workhouse had a low entrance block, behind which stood the T-shaped main building. Its rear wing contained a dining-hall on the ground floor with a chapel above. Four pavilion ward blocks lay at the rear.

Prestwich Union effectively ceased to exist in 1915 when it was (re-)amalgamated with Manchester and came under the control on the Manchester Board of Guardians.

In 1918, the former Prestwich workhouse became Delaunay's Road Institution, later Delaunay's Hospital, which in turn became part of the North Manchester General Hospital. Nothing of the buildings now survives. (MAN)

ROCHDALE

Rochdale's township workhouses included Spotland (SD887136), Hollingworth (SD943148), Marland (SD879120), Calf Hey (SD914173) and Wardleworth (SD896140).

Rochdale was prominent amongst the northern areas opposed to the New Poor Law. Despite opposition from local ratepayers, the Rochdale Union was created on 15 February 1837.

Radical opponents of the 1834 Act, led by Thomas Livesey, first attempted to boycott Guardians' elections. They then put up their own candidates who, when elected, did not attend Board meetings. Mounting pressure from the PLC finally led, in 1845, to legal action being instituted against members of the Board of Guardians. Although the prosecution failed due to a legal technicality, the Commissioners persuaded local magistrates, who were ex officio members

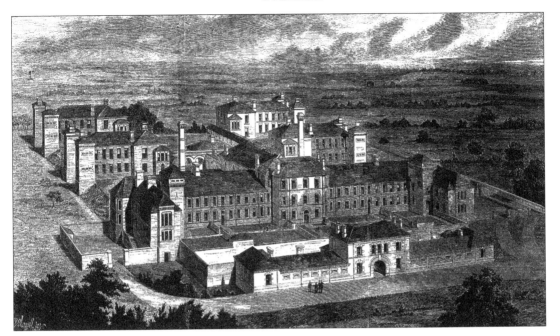

An 1872 bird's-eye view of the new Prestwich workhouse, designed by Thomas Worthington. The entrance and probationary block in the foreground is separated by walled yards from the main building which had light, airy corridors. Sick wards lay either side of a garden area at the rear of the site.

of the Board, to begin conducting union business. In April 1846, a new Board was elected and was dominated by anti-Poor Law members who continued to obstruct the Poor Law authorities.

In 1863, a new union workhouse was erected at Marland (SD878118) to replace the old Marland and Calf Hey buildings. It was built by unemployed cotton workers during the American Civil War, as a Poor Law project, to provide paid employment.

An official inspection in 1870 criticised Marland's very poor provision for the sick. Medicines were administered by paupers who could not read and kept in unlabeled bottles, together with blacking and firewood, in a box. Although pauper nurses had to be able to read, the Guardians claimed that the medical officer never wrote prescriptions because the only medicine in the unlabeled bottles was cod-liver oil, as the illiterate nurses well knew. All inmates urinated into a tub in the corner of each ward – the urine was sold by the Guardians for scouring cotton. Diarrhoea was endemic.

In 1886, the Marland workhouse was converted for use as an infectious diseases hospital, later becoming Marland Hospital, and providing geriatric care into the 1970s. It is now demolished.

In 1871, the union purchased a 24-acre site on Birch Hill at Dearnley (SD921160) on which to erect a new workhouse. Early in 1874, the Spotland workhouse partially collapsed. However, because the Dearnley building was still unfinished, it had to be patched up and used for a further four years.

The new workhouse opened in December 1877. The total cost of the buildings and land was a massive £85,000. The main block was dominated by a large clock/water tower. At the centre of the building were the Master's quarters, with the dining-hall (also originally used as a chapel) and kitchen and bakehouse behind. Male inmates were placed at the west, and females to the east.

The uphill trudge to Rochdale's new union workhouse at Dearnley. It was opened by Alderman T. Schofield on 19 December 1877. Seventy guests attended the ceremony which was followed by a tour of the premises and dinner at 3 p.m. Afterwards, there were long speeches, and a performance by the Orpheus Glee Club.

A 1908 view of Rochdale Union's cottage homes at Wardle, erected in 1898. The site was requisitioned at the outbreak of the Second World War in 1939. All the buildings have now been demolished.

In 1902, a 172-bed pavilion-plan infirmary was built at the north of the workhouse.

During the First World War, the military used part of the site and erected tents in the grounds. In 1930, the site passed to Rochdale County Borough and in 1948 became Birch Hill Hospital. The hospital has now closed and much of the site is being redeveloped as housing.

In 1898, Rochdale erected a children's cottage homes site at Wardle (SD920169). (LAN)

SALFORD

Salford had at least two pre-1834 workhouses – one in the Greengate district (SJ834990), just across the Irwell from the centre of Manchester, the other at Pendleton (SJ812995) on the east side of what is now Broughton Road.

Salford was a centre of resistance to the 1834 Poor Law Act and a Salford Anti-Poor Law Movement was formed led by the Chartist R.J. Richardson. The Board of Guardians refused to co-operate with the PLC and continued using the old and inadequate workhouse buildings at Greengate and Pendleton until a new workhouse was eventually built in 1853. The Greengate building was then replaced by the Collier Street public baths designed by Thomas Worthington, architect of Chorlton workhouse infirmary.

The new workhouse (SJ809982) was on an elongated site between the busy Eccles New Road and the Manchester to Liverpool railway. The building was designed in the Elizabethan style by Pennington & Jarvis and was intended to accommodate 300 inmates. A two-storey block containing offices and receiving wards fronted on to the main road. To its rear was the imposing 400-feet-long main building which, according to one report, had 'an arcade entrance of polished Yorkshire stone, surmounted by a trellis battlement, cut and moulded. The central portion is three, and the wings two stories high: the roofs are high-pitched, and have projecting gables and carved barge boards. On the centre of the building there rises a clock tower, with an octagon shaft.'

The workhouse closed after the First World War and the building was demolished soon after the abolition of the Board of Guardians in 1930. It was replaced by the three-storey flats of the Langworthy Estate, a large-scale rehousing project, which was officially opened in 1938.

In 1882, the union opened an 880-bed infirmary at the south side of Eccles Old Road at Hope. In 1924-5, a large and innovative complex of homes for 500 elderly people was built alongside the infirmary. The site is now the home of Hope Hospital, but few of the old buildings remain. In 1903, the union erected a cottage homes scheme for 300 children at Culcheth (SJ650960). (SAL)

TOXTETH PARK

The parish of Toxteth Park, originally part of the populous West Derby Union, became an independent Poor Law Parish in 1857.

In 1858-9, the union built a large new workhouse on Smithdown Road in Toxteth (SJ378888). It was designed by William Culshaw who was also the architect of the workhouses at Ormskirk and Belmont Road, West Derby.

In 1922, Toxteth Park was absorbed by the West Derby Union. The workhouse later became Smithdown Road Institution and then Sefton General Hospital. In 2001, a major redevelopment of the site removed virtually all the old workhouse buildings. (LIV)

ULVERSTON

In 1753, Neville Hall (SD284784) was purchased for the sum of £163 3s for use as a poorhouse by the parish of Ulverston. Another early workhouse was at Billincoat (or Billing Cate, SD226726) in the parish of Dalton which opened in 1735. In 1826, the Dalton parish workhouse moved to a new site at Goose Green (SD225737), some of whose buildings still survive. The parish of Colton (or Coulton) erected a workhouse at Backbarrow in 1823 at a cost of £250.

The new Ulverston Union workhouse was built in 1838 at the north-west of the town on the west side of Stanley Street (SD284786), at a cost of £5,800. A small infirmary appears to have been added in around 1868, although this was later demolished, probably to make way for the separate children's accommodation at the west of the site. In 1887, after a recent enlargement, the workhouse could accommodate 282 inmates.

After 1948, the former workhouse became known as Stanley Hospital, then after the closure and demolition of the Ulverston Hospital in 1971, it adopted the name Ulverston Hospital. The site has now been redeveloped and the old buildings removed. (CUB)

WARRINGTON

Warrington's first workhouse was erected on Church Street in 1728 and accommodated around 100 inmates. The rules of the house in 1820 included the barring of alcohol, no spitting or filth of any kind, no profane swearing, cursing or 'obscene jests'. There was also a ban on the 'reading of songs, ballads, books or publications of an immoral tendency'. Eden, in his 1797 survey of the poor in England, described the workhouse in Warrington as having:

> ... 95 inmates (50 children under 9 years and the rest mostly old and infirm). They are employed in spinning hair for hair cloth, winding warp for sailcloth, etc. Half the heavy sailcloth used in the Navy was made here. The Workhouse is an old one, but is kept very clean, and the Poor there seem very contented.

After its formation in 1837, the new Warrington Union took over existing township workhouses at Warrington (SJ613883) and on Bridge Street in Newton-le-Willows (SJ576952).

A new union workhouse was built in 1849-51 on the east side of Lovely Lane in Warrington (SJ596888). The main building was a long two-storey block with cross wings at each end. A dining hall, kitchens and chapel were located at the rear. In around 1898, a large infirmary was built to the north of the workhouse.

The workhouse later became Whitecross Institution and subsequently Warrington District General Hospital.

In 1880-1, the union opened 'industrial schools' at Padgate (SJ636897) for its children.

WEST DERBY

Formed in 1837, West Derby was a large union surrounding Liverpool which itself was constituted as separate Poor Law Parish. Prior to this date, small workhouses in operation included Allerton, Childwall and Wavertree.

West Derby Poor Law Union's first workhouse was built on Mill Road in the Everton district (SJ363915) in 1840. By 1866, Poor Law Inspector R.B. Cane described it as 'wholly insufficient for the wants of the union'. In 1867, the buildings were converted to become the St George's Catholic Industrial School. The site was redeveloped in 1891-93 for use as an infirmary, later becoming Mill Road Maternity Hospital. Housing now occupies the site.

In 1864-9, a new workhouse was built on Rice Lane at Walton-on-the-Hill (SJ358954) to serve the north of the union. Walton originally accommodated 1,200 inmates and its construction cost £65,000. It gradually expanded and by 1930 could house 2,500.

The workhouse later became Walton Institution and then Walton Hospital, now closed.

In 1889-90, a 'test' workhouse was built at Belmont Road (SJ372924), providing daily out-relief

Salford's Culcheth cottage homes included thirteen double cottages, schools, a superintendent's house and an infirmary. The picture shows a training block and swimming baths (right). The site produced its own bread, electricity, water and heat. The shoemaking, joinery and painting shops kept both boots and buildings in good repair.

The main building of Toxteth Park's Smithdown Road workhouse was around 500 feet in length and three storeys high, with a large clock tower at its centre.

The entrance to the former Ulverston workhouse – one of the few northern workhouses to be based on the Poor Law Commissioners' model cruciform design.

Warrington's Industrial School at Padgate was later redesignated as a cottage homes site, perhaps reflecting a change in the age range of its inmates. The buildings included two boys' houses, two girls' houses, play-sheds, a school, superintendent's house and porter's lodge. The site is now a business park.

A 1925 view of the Walton-on-the-Hill workhouse. The main building was a long three-storey T-shaped block, with males housed at the east and females at the west. The workhouse grounds covered 37 acres, much of it cultivated to provide useful employment for the inmates.

A view from around 1900 of the West Derby Cottage Homes at Fazakerley taken by the then Superintendent, W.J. Guilbert. This scene shows some of the young inmates in front of the homes' swimming pool which is still in use.

in return for manual work such as stone-breaking. The Belmont Road workhouse later became Newsham General Hospital. Virtually all the buildings have been demolished.

West Derby Union operated a number of other establishments, including cottage homes at Fazakerley (SJ388975) and the Alder Hey Hospital (SJ404919), which originally catered for the chronic sick before becoming a children's hospital. (LIV)

WIGAN

In 1777, a parliamentary survey recorded parish workhouses in operation in Wigan (for up to 200 inmates), Dalton (twenty), Pemberton (sixty), and Standish with Langtree (forty).

In 1837, the new Wigan Union at first made use of existing workhouse buildings on Frog Lane at the west of Wigan (SD574060), and on the Liverpool Road to the south of Hindley (SD613039).

In 1855-7, a new union workhouse was erected on the Frog Lane site. The buildings were constructed in red brick and accommodated 574 inmates.

From 1930, the former workhouse became Frog Lane Public Assistance Institution providing care for the elderly and chronic sick. After the setting up of the NHS in 1948, it became Frog Lane Welfare Home and later Frog Lane Hospital. It finally closed in around 1970. The buildings were demolished in the 1990s and housing now occupies the site.

In 1906, the union opened a poor law infirmary at the east side of Upholland Road (SD528028). The hospital later became Wigan's Billinge Hospital, finally closing in 2004. (WIG, LAN)

CHAPTER 4

NORTHUMBERLAND

The rear of Alnwick's main block showing the women's wing (left), Master's quarters (centre), and dining-hall (right). The former workhouse buildings were later used as an old people's home. The main building has now been converted to offices.

ALNWICK

By the 1770s, workhouses were in operation at Alnwick, Birling and Warkworth. A workhouse opened in 1810 in Alnwick, on a site between Roxburgh Place and Hotspur Street (NU188132). In 1814, twenty of its inmates had ages totalling 1,523 years, an average of seventy-six years – said to be a testimony to 'the salubrity of the air of Alnwick'.

The Alnwick Union was formed in 1836 and in 1841 opened a new workhouse for 120 inmates on Wagonway Road in Alnwick (NU190128). Its main building was a T-shaped block with a dining-hall in its rear wing. An infirmary and mortuary lay west of the main workhouse. Buildings to the south of the workhouse included the Master's house and a children's block.

After 1930, the workhouse became Alnwick Public Assistance Institution, accommodating chronic sick patients. In 1941, Alnwick received inmates from the institutions at Hexham and Ponteland which were preparing to receive war casualties. However, Alnwick closed in 1943 and its inmates moved out to the Thomas Taylor village homes near Stannington. (NOR)

BELFORD

Belford Union's workhouse, one of the smallest in the country, was built in 1838–9 on West Street in Belford (NU107338). Originally the Guardians had proposed a building for twenty-five inmates (rather less than the PLC's normal minimum of fifty) which they felt was perfectly adequate for the likely demand. Eventually a modest single-storey T-shaped building for thirty was agreed, capable of being enlarged with an extra storey. The Guardians appear to have been justified – in 1866 the workhouse never had more than twenty-six in residence. A separate infirmary block was erected to the east of the main building in 1874. The establishment was run entirely by the Master, Matron and a paid porter although the low salaries offered by the Guardians often caused problems in retaining staff.

In recent years, the buildings were used as a social services day centre. but have now all been demolished. (NOR)

Bellingham was more typical of local farmhouses than any of the standard workhouse designs. The building, later known as Fountain Cottage, was enlarged in 1874 and 'reconditioned' in 1937. A block to the rear may have been an infirmary. Outbuildings to the north were probably vagrants' accommodation.

Berwick's Castlegate workhouse – access was via a narrow alley from the somewhat ironically named Featherbed Lane (now Brucegate) to the east.

The Glendale Union workhouse is now home to the Cheviot Centre, providing facilities for the local community and tourists. A permanent display celebrates the life of Josephine Butler, the Glendale-born Victorian social reformer. She spent much of her time trying to improve the conditions in workhouses for women.

BELLINGHAM

Otterburn Ward and Rochester both had workhouses in operation by the 1770s.

The Bellingham Union workhouse was built in 1839 at the north side of Bellingham (NY839835). The building accommodated fifty-three inmates although rarely had more than half that number.

The building is now owned by the local district council and houses a tea-shop, tourist information office and library. (NOR)

BERWICK-UPON-TWEED

In the 1770s, Tweedmouth had a workhouse for up to thirty-six inmates. Parson and White's 1827 directory noted that Berwick's workhouse 'often contains about 1,000 inmates. It stands in a healthy situation in Castlegate, & was formerly used as a sacking manufactory, but it is now fitted up in a comfortable & commodious manner for its present purpose, & has a school attached to it, for the education of the pauper children, & also a Lunatic Asylum built in 1813.'

The Berwick-upon-Tweed Union, created in November 1836, took over the existing Castlegate premises (NT997534). The building had a main H-shaped block with a separate block at the west housing the hospital, vagrants' wards and boys' school. In 1866, the boys' and girls' schools had a total of seven pupils from the workhouse, together with eighty pauper children from outside.

The former workhouse later became a geriatric hospital linked with the nearby Berwick Infirmary. In 2001, the surviving buildings were redeveloped for use as housing. (NOR)

CASTLE WARD

By the 1770s, Heddon-on-the-Wall had a local workhouse for up to fifty inmates.

Castle Ward Union, created in September 1836, initially took over the old Heddon-on-the-Wall workhouse. A new building was subsequently erected at Ponteland (NZ165733) in 1848. Designed by John and Benjamin Green, it accommodated about 120 inmates although rarely exceeded sixty.

The workhouse later became Ponteland Poor Law Institution and then Ponteland Hospital. The buildings were demolished in the late 1990s and the site is now occupied by a housing development which, appropriately, is called Guardians Court. (NOR)

GLENDALE

Pre-1800 workhouses existed in Carham Parish and Wooler Parish.

After its formation in 1836, the Glendale Union erected a workhouse for seventy inmates at the south of Wooler High Street (NT989281). The two-storey building, which cost around £1,500, had a cruciform layout with the Master and Matron's quarters at the centre. In the 1850s, extra male accommodation was erected above the vagrants' ward. In 1866, an inspector described the rooms as 'limited in size, and low'. The Master acted as schoolmaster for both boys and girls, most of whom were resident outside.

The building was used from 1894-1954 as the headquarters of Glendale Rural District Council and was thereafter used as an archaeology centre and then as a Field Study Centre.

The building has been refurbished as the Cheviot Centre. (NOR)

HALTWHISTLE

A parliamentary return in 1777 recorded workhouses in operation at Bellister (for up to eighty inmates), Blenkinsopp (eighty), Coanwood (forty), Fetherstone (forty), Plenmeller (eighty), Thirlwall (eighty) and Walltown (forty-two).

Haltwhistle Poor Law Union was formed in October 1836 and erected a workhouse on Greenholme Road at the west of Haltwhistle (NY704641). Although it could only accommodate

One of Hexham workhouse's sick wards – now used as offices. In 1866, a report on the children's accommodation at the workhouse noted that 'the boys sometimes dig and plant the garden; the girls sew and knit, and the elder assist in milking and churning, for which purpose two cows are kept.'

up to sixty inmates, it was rarely more than half full – during 1866 it never had more than twenty-two in residence.

The site was later known as Greenholme Institution. The buildings no longer exist. (NOR)

HEXHAM

Parson and White's 1827 directory noted of Hexham that: 'The Workhouse is at the head of Priest-popple, where Mrs Mary Hutchinson, the governess, supports each pauper at the rate of 2s 6d per head weekly. The poor of other parishes are taken in on the same terms, by paying an additional sum, not exceeding two guineas, yearly.' Corbridge workhouse was described as 'a plain building, situated in Watling-street, where Mr. James Bowman presides as governor.'

Hexham Poor Law Union was created in October 1836 and in 1839 erected a new workhouse on Dean Street at the east of Hexham (NY941640). Major reconstruction work in 1883 included new sick wards and a Master's house at the west of the site.

After 1930, the workhouse became Hexham Public Assistance Institution. During the Second World War, the buildings were requisitioned for administrative use. After 1948, the site became part of Hexham General Hospital. The older buildings are now used for administrative purposes. (NOR)

MORPETH

Morpeth's first workhouse may have been the almshouses on Cottingwood Lane (NZ197864). A later town workhouse stood on Newgate Street (NZ197862).

The Morpeth Poor Law Union, formed in September 1836, initially continued using the old Newgate Street workhouse. A new building for 150 inmates was erected on the same site in 1865-7. The architect was Frederick R. Wilson.

The buildings were used as county council offices during the Second World War, then demolished in 1951 and replaced by a telephone exchange. (NOR)

In the First World War, the military authorities took over all the Newcastle workhouse buildings, and some of the hospital for the treatment of venereal diseases in soldiers. In 1939, at the start of the Second World War, the western part of the entrance building and the entrance archway were taken down in case of bombing.

Rothbury's old parish workhouse (right of centre), which still stands on Town Head, was used by the Rothbury Union for over sixty years.

The new Rothbury Union workhouse opened in 1902. In 1905, the Rothbury Board of Guardians invited tenders for a water supply to the building. A guest house now operates in the premises.

NEWCASTLE-UPON-TYNE

In 1831, there were four parish workhouses in Newcastle: St Nicholas', adjoining Long Stairs opened in 1803 and had thirty-six inmates; St John's in Bath Lane, adjoining the Lunatic Asylum, housed thirty-five; St Andrew's housed fifty-six inmates; and All Saints, which occupied part of the site of the Augustine Convent and was previously used as a general hospital for the poor of Newcastle.

The Newcastle-upon-Tyne Union was created in September 1836. In 1839, the Guardians decided to replace the existing old workhouses with a new one at the top of Westgate Hill (NZ228645). The first buildings, at the junction of Westgate Road and Brighton Grove, included an administration block, dining-hall, laundry, bakehouse, workshops, school, sick wards, lying-in ward and imbeciles' ward. Males were housed at the west of the workhouse and females at the east.

In December 1870, a large U-shaped infirmary was opened at the west of the site. A separate children's block was erected between the workhouse and the infirmary, with boys housed in the northern part of the building, and girls and infants at the south. A separate block contained the children's swimming bath. In 1902, after the children were moved to new cottage homes at Ponteland (NZ154741), the buildings were used for the workhouse's aged and infirm inmates. In 1882, an imposing three-storey entrance building with a central archway replaced the old lodge.

The former workhouse site now forms part of Newcastle General Hospital.

Newcastle had a large cottage homes site at Ponteland (NZ155740). The union also sent boys to the training ship *Wellesley* moored on the Tyne at North Shields (TAW)

ROTHBURY

By 1775, workhouses were in operation at Rothbury and Whitton. Rothbury's parish workhouse was on Town Foot (NU061018).

After its formation in October 1836, Rothbury Poor Law Union took over the existing Town Foot workhouse. In 1901, the Guardians purchased a site to the south of Rothbury on Silverton Lane (NU063012) and erected a new workhouse for fifty inmates and a school. The main building was a two-storey block with the Master and Matron's accommodation at the centre, men's day room and dormitories to the east, and women's to the west. To the rear was a single-storey block containing a wash-house, laundry, kitchen, shed and mortuary.

By 1941, the establishment had been renamed Silverton House and was a home for forty-five young mental defectives, including fourteen epileptics. The buildings were derelict from the 1960s until 1988 but have now been converted into residential and guest-house accommodation. (NOR)

TYNEMOUTH

Tynemouth had a parish workhouse on Preston Lane (now Preston Road) in North Shields. Parson and White's 1827 directory recorded that the establishment:

> … is an extensive building, pleasantly situated at a short distance north of the church. The expenditure of this house, for the year ending December, 1826, was £898 8s. 6¾d., and the average number of inmates, during the last four years, has been about 90, and their maintenance has cost their respective townships about 3s. 9d. per head weekly.

After its formation in September 1836, Tynemouth Poor Law Union continued to use the existing Preston Lane workhouse. Then, in 1848, a new union workhouse was erected, also on Preston Lane (NZ354689). It was substantially rebuilt and enlarged in 1886-9 after the acquisition of the cricket ground to the north. New infirmary blocks were added in 1903 and 1909, followed by an operating theatre in 1913, mortuary in 1920, and receiving wards in 1925-6.

In 1930, the workhouse became Tynemouth Public Assistance Institution, and subsequently Preston Hospital. The site has been completely redeveloped for housing. (TAW)

CHAPTER 5

WESTMORLAND

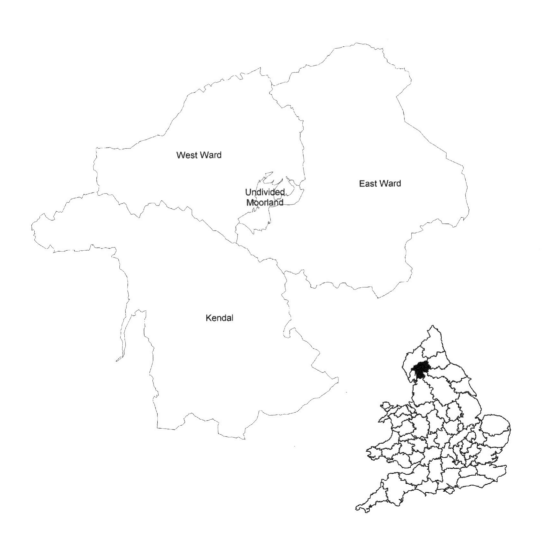

EAST WARD

Kirkby Stephen and seven other parishes united under the terms of Gilbert's Act of 1782. In 1810, the union set up a workhouse in a former cotton mill in Kirkby Stephen to the north of St Stephen's church.

After its formation in October 1836, the East Ward Union took over and enlarged the existing workhouse at Kirkby Stephen (NY776089). A report in 1866 described the workhouse as an old and dilapidated building with very low rooms and where the classification and arrangements were very imperfect.

After 1930, the workhouse became a Public Assistance Institution known as Eden House providing accommodation for the chronic sick and what were then termed 'Part III' or healthy destitute inmates.

The workhouse buildings no longer exist and the site has been redeveloped for housing. When tthis closed, the site was sold to the Shap Granite Company as housing for its workforce. (CUK)

KENDAL

In 1769, Kendal erected a workhouse on Stricklandgate (SD513933). There were also two Gilbert Union workhouses in the area. Kirkby Lonsdale formed a union with sixteen other parishes and erected a workhouse on Mill Brow (SD613788) in 1811. In 1813, a union comprising Milnthorpe, Heversham and fifteen other townships built a workhouse at Milnthorpe (SD505818).

In 1836, the new Kendal Poor Law Union took over the Stricklandgate workhouse, which was used for able-bodied men and children over seven years, while the Milnthorpe workhouse was used to house the aged and infirm, infants, able-bodied women and unmarried mothers.

In 1861, the Stricklandgate workhouse was described as:

> ...a large, uniform building, two stories high, occupying three sides of a quadrangle, the fourth, which is the entrance, being open to the street. It contains, for the purposes of the paupers, one large general dining-room, kitchens, store-rooms, sick-rooms, &c. on the first floor; and on the second floor thirty-five well-ventilated lodging-rooms, which contain eighty-nine good beds, supplied with sufficient comfortable clothing, and capable of accommodating two hundred persons; together with suitable apartments appropriated to the use of the governor and his family. A productive garden is attached to the Workhouse, cultivated by the labour of the inmates.

The Kendal workhouse was later known as Windermere Road Institution, then after 1948 became Kendal Green Hospital until its closure in 1970. The surviving buildings have now been converted to housing. (CUK)

WEST WARD

After its formation in September 1836, the West Ward Union took over the former Gilbert Union workhouse at Eamont Bridge (NY523286). Like the neighbouring East Ward Union, the workhouse was criticised in 1866, particularly in its provision for sick and infectious cases. The building was said to be old and most unsuitable for the purpose and the construction of a new workhouse was strongly recommended.

This took place in 1877 when a new building was erected on Home Lane at Shap (NY564142). The premises were later used as a children's home by the Carlisle Union. (CUK)

Kendal's Stricklandgate workhouse. Local people recall that in the early 1900s, groups of paupers sat on Kendal Green (just north-west of the workhouse) breaking huge stones brought by cart from the quarries. They sat there winter and summer, and when it rained they covered themselves with sacks.

The Milnthorpe Gilbert Union workhouse, later used by Kendal Union, was erected in 1813 at a cost of £4,990 and designed by Francis Webster of Kendal. It featured a semi-hub at its centre – a very early example of such a feature.

Kirkby Lonsdale formed a Gilbert Union with sixteen other townships and erected a workhouse in 1811 at a cost of £2,500. After the creation of the Kendal Union the building was later used to house vagrants.

The West Ward Union workhouse site at Shap was later sold to the local Shap Granite Company as housing for their workforce.

CHAPTER 6

YORKSHIRE – EAST RIDING

BEVERLEY

The joint parish of St Mary and St Nicholas together with St Martin operated a combined workhouse from 1727 until 1795 when the premises were divided in two.

After the formation of the Beverley Union in November 1836, the Guardians declined to build a new workhouse but made use of an existing building on the south side of Minster Moor Gate in Beverley (TA036392). However, in 1860-61, a new building for 189 inmates was erected at Westwood (TA027395). In 1894, a sixty-bed infirmary was added, together with casual wards for forty-one vagrants.

The workhouse later became Beverley Institution, then Westwood Hospital. (YER)

BRIDLINGTON

Prior to 1834, local workhouses existed on Church Green in Bridlington, and at Hunmanby.

The new Bridlington Union, created in October 1836, at first declined to build a new workhouse but continued using the existing Church Green workhouse in Bridlington. However, in 1846, a new building for 150 inmates was erected on Marton Road (TA175681), at a cost of about £6,000. The building included two single-storey entrance lodges and a cruciform main block which accommodated males at the east and females at the west. Short cross-wings housed boys' and girls' schools. An infirmary lay at the south of the workhouse.

The workhouse later became the Avenue Hospital and was used as children's summer holiday accommodation. It was later renamed Burlington House and provided geriatric care. (YER)

DRIFFIELD

Driffield had a small workhouse at the south side of Cross Hill (TA023577) dating from 1742. Other local workhouses existed at Hutton Cranswick, Kilham, Nafferton and North Dalton.

After its creation in 1836, the Driffield Union briefly carried on using the Cross Hill and Nafferton premises. In 1837 it acquired vacant land called 'Promise Close' between Westgate and Middle Street in Driffield (TA021581) on which to build a new workhouse.

An official inspection of the workhouse in 1866 criticised the absence of work for vagrants. On the first night that a work task was introduced, twelve of the sixteen male vagrants applying for admission declined to enter; the other four left the next day informing the Master that they would not trouble him again.

In 1866-8, a new building for 215 inmates was erected on Bridlington Road in Driffield (TA033585). The entrance block at the south contained the board-room, offices and chapel. At the rear stood the three-storey main building, behind which lay the kitchens and dining-hall. An infirmary lay at the north of the site. The Driffield vagrants' ward provided neither food nor baths, apparently because it was felt that such luxuries would encourage vagrancy.

The workhouse later became a treatment centre for TB. Under the NHS it became the East Riding County Hospital, and more recently was a private hospital. Housing now occupies the site. (YER)

HOWDEN

From 1665-1794, a site on Pinfold Street in Howden (SE746281) was used as a lodging house for the needy. A workhouse was then opened on the site which included a manufactory, stone-breaking yard, cowshed and prison. There were other township workhouses at Cave and at Holme-on-Spalding-Moor (SE809368) whose facilities included a small circular 'lock-up'.

In 1837, the new Howden Union originally decided to continue using existing workhouses in Howden, Holme and Cave. However, in 1839, the Guardians were persuaded to erect a new building which was located on the south side of Knedlington Road (SE743280).

The fine main building of Beverley's union workhouse, built in 1861 at a cost of £5,500. The red-brick Tudor-style design was by John and William Atkinson of York, who were architects of more than a dozen Yorkshire workhouses, including those at Howden, Pocklington and Skirlaugh.

The main block of Howden's workhouse was a deep oblong structure with a short central wing at the rear, dividing male and female sides, with observation windows in the angled corners. This 1920s picture appears to show some maintenance taking place, supervised perhaps by the Master.

The 'inner court' of Hull's Anlaby Road workhouse in around 1904. After the opening ceremony on 30 June 1852, 280 paupers were transferred from the old Charity Hall workhouse and given a celebratory dinner of roast beef, mutton, plum pudding, tea, and spice cake.

After 1930, the workhouse later became Howden Public Assistance Institution, and then Howden Hospital. It finally closed in 1947 and was later demolished. (YER)

KINGSTON-UPON-HULL

(Kingston-upon-) Hull formed a Local Act Incorporation in 1698 and erected a building at 51 Whitefriargate known as Charity Hall (TA098287). Work for the inmates included oakum picking and spinning. Any inmate who 'shall curse or swear or be in liquor' was confined to the stocks for up to four hours, while any child found to 'take God's name in vain or use any profane language… shall stand on a stool in the dining-hall during the times of dinner, with the crime written in large letters on a paper, which shall be pinned on their breasts and they shall only have bread and water that day.' A later writer circumspectly reported that 'certain single women coming to the house through their own misconduct had their names entered in a book, had meat rations stopped and had to wear coarse yellow coats or gowns, or other disgraceful distinctions. Women coming to the house a second time for medical aid had to stand in the pillory in the workhouse yard for an hour at least and then be confined in one of the small rooms at the bottom of the yard.'

Its Local Act status made Hull largely immune from the 1834 Poor Law Act, although the parishes surrounding Hull did fall in line and formed the Sculcoates Poor Law Union.

In 1850, there was a scandal involving a pregnant woman being refused admission to the workhouse and promptly giving birth on the workhouse steps. This, together with criticisms of conditions in Charity Hall, led to the construction in 1851–2 of a new building for 600 inmates on Anlaby Road (TA084288). The Italianate-style design comprised entrance buildings with offices and casual wards, and a main block with accommodation wards, 550-seat dining-hall, kitchen and school. To the rear were a dining-hall, 400-seat chapel and an infirmary. Later additions to the site included the East Hospital in 1892, and the Naval Hospital or West Hospital in 1914.

Now the site of Hull Royal Infirmary, little remains of the former workhouse buildings. (HUL)

PATRINGTON

A parish workhouse existed at Patrington from 1806. The workhouse inmates were hired out for use as farm labour.

The Patrington Poor Law Union was formed in September 1836 and erected a workhouse on Station Road (TA311228). It was a rectangular brick structure accommodating 120 inmates. A new eighteen-bed infirmary block was opened in March 1903, at cost of £2,000.

Discipline was strict in the workhouse – according to the Pauper Offence Book, 'disorderly' girls were flogged by the Matron.

The establishment was finally closed on 18 January 1947. The building was later used as a factory but was demolished in 1981. (YER)

POCKLINGTON

In 1777, Pocklington was recorded as having a workhouse accommodating up to twelve inmates.

The new Pocklington Poor Law Union was formed in October 1836. Apart from Hull, Pocklington was East Riding's only centre of opposition to the 1834 Poor Law Act. The union refused to erect a central workhouse, and retained an old workhouse on Hungate at Market Weighton (SE879418) which was described as 'a quadrangular range of small cottages of one apartment in height with a moderate-sized yard at the centre.' The premises were eventually closed down in 1851 following a cholera outbreak. The union then agreed to erect a new workhouse for 113 inmates, situated at the south-east of the town (SE806488) on the road to Burnby. It was a brick structure and its construction cost £1,608 plus £360 for the land on which it stood. A hospital was added in 1878.

'Not many passengers along the Beverley-road would imagine that the beautiful and immense structure which is in course of erection, on ground just beyond the town, is intended for the reception of paupers. Its front aspect would not disgrace the residence of a nobleman.' – the *Hull Advertiser*'s 1844 report on the new Sculcoates workhouse.

Skirlaugh's workhouse was designed by the prolific John and William Atkinson. After its closure in 1915, the children and few remaining inmates were removed to Beverley. The following year, the workhouse took on the role of a military hospital.

York's new union workhouse had three main sections: an entrance block at the east, a hospital block to the west, and the main block at the centre. The main block, shown here, was said to deliberately resemble a mill.

After the Second World War, the former workhouse became The Poplars old people's home but was demolished in the mid-1970s. (YER)

SCULCOATES

In 1823, Sculcoates had a parish workhouse on Wilson's Row, Wincolmlee (TA099296). Another was located at Drypool, at the east of the River Hull.

The Sculcoates Union, formed in 1837, erected a workhouse for 500 inmates at the east side of the Beverley Road (TA091301). An 1844 account in the *Hull Advertiser* described it as follows:

> …it is in a plain Gothic style, and of an extent far greater than that of any other edifice in or near Hull. Its width is 260 feet, and it extends 370 feet from the front to the back. In the centre of the immense building are the rooms appropriated to the governor, the matron, etc. On each side of these rooms are the day-rooms for the male and female paupers of every class. Behind the centre buildings is the dining-room, capable of seating 300 persons; and adjoining this room are the kitchens. The sleeping-rooms are above the day-rooms of the paupers, and to each class of pauper is appropriated a spacious and airy court. Near to the main buildings are the school-rooms, wash-houses, tailors' shops, shoemakers' shops, and all the buildings necessary for an establishment of this great extent. The infirmary is at the extremity of the ground, as are the gig-houses and stables for the guardians; there is a good extent of garden ground beyond the buildings. The front of the edifice consists of a board-room, clerks' rooms, relieving officers' rooms and waiting rooms. The paupers' rooms are spacious, light and airy; and they command a prospect which would be envied by many of our wealthy inhabitants residing in the town.

The workhouse later became the Beverley Road Institution and, after 1948, Kingston General Hospital. The buildings were demolished in 2002 and a school now stands on the site.

In 1897, Sculcoates erected a cottage homes development at Hessle (TA043266). (HUL)

SKIRLAUGH

Formed on October 1836, the new Skirlaugh Union erected a workhouse in 1838-9 at the west side of the main road running north from Skirlaugh (TA138399). The buildings, a graceful Classical design by J. & W. Atkinson, cost £2,332 and accommodated around sixty inmates.

The Skirlaugh workhouse closed in 1915. In 1922, it was acquired for use as offices by Holderness Borough Council, afterwards the East Riding of Yorkshire Council, and renamed Rowton Villas. (YER)

YORK

A small parish workhouse for ninety paupers existed at 26 Marygate in York (SE598522).

The York Poor Law Union was formed in July 1837 and took over the existing Marygate site. However, by 1845 it was overcrowded and unsanitary, and the PLC strongly recommended the construction of a replacement. In September 1847, the Guardians agreed to build a new workhouse for 300 inmates. Its design was opened to competition with the winning entry coming from local architects J.B. & W. Atkinson. The building, which cost under £6,000, was completed in 1849 at a site on Huntington Road (SE608530).

In 1930, the workhouse became York Public Assistance Institution, then in 1946 was renamed the Grange Hospital. In 1955 it was renamed St Mary's Hospital to avoid confusion with The Grange old people's institution. The hospital closed in the late 1970s and the buildings have now been converted to student accommodation. (YRK)

CHAPTER 7

YORKSHIRE – NORTH RIDING

AYSGARTH / BAINBRIDGE

In April 1813, Bainbridge and seven other parishes formed a Gilbert Union. The union operated a workhouse at the west of Bainbridge (SD933901) which accommodated about sixty inmates.

Its Gilbert Union status exempted Bainbridge from many of the provisions of the 1834 Poor Law Amendment Act. Despite pressure from the PLC for it to convert to a Poor Law Union within the 1834 Act, it remained in operation until 1869 when all remaining Gilbert Unions were abolished. It was replaced by the Aysgarth Poor Law Union which took over the existing workhouse at Bainbridge.

The premises are now used as a care home for the elderly. (NRY)

BEDALE

The parishes of Bedale and Aiskew had poorhouses from at least 1776. The buildings were adapted from cottages or farmhouses and were poorly suited for the purpose.

Bedale originally became part of the Northallerton Poor Law Union. However, a number of influential local landowners and magistrates felt that Bedale should be the centre of its own union. Twelve Guardians representing the Bedale district disrupted the Northallerton Board's business to such an extent that in 1839 a new Bedale Union was created which included parishes previously falling within the Thirsk and Leyburn Unions.

A Bedale Union workhouse was erected in 1839 at South End in Bedale (SE269879). The architects were J. & W. Atkinson of York.

In the 1930s, the building became Mowbray Grange TB Sanatorium then later Mowbray Grange Hospital. The site was sold off in 1991 and has been converted to residential use. (NRY)

EASINGWOLD

Easingwold had a parish workhouse from at least 1756. It was situated on Uppleby (SE531701) and housed thirty inmates. Its regime in 1829 was fairly severe, with men, women and children strictly segregated, fires lit only by order of the Vestry, and candles provided only for the sick. Work was from 7 a.m. (8 a.m. in winter) to 6 p.m. with male inmates grinding corn and women doing domestic work. The food, however, was relatively good with four meat dinners a week.

Easingwold Poor Law Union, established in February 1837, erected a workhouse for 130 inmates on Oulston Road (SE534704). It cost about £2,600 and was designed by the prolific J. & W. Atkinson of York. The compact building had a two-storey central block with three-storey wings.

In 1934, the former workhouse was converted to become Claypenny 'Colony' and provided care for up to 200 people with learning disabilities.

The surviving buildings have now been converted to housing. (NRY)

GUISBOROUGH

In 1777, workhouses operated at Guisborough, Marske and Skelton. Guisborough's was said to be 'an old tumbledown cottage'. A paid manager was employed but it appears not to have been a popular job. One lame pauper seeking relief was 'offered' the post under threat of his allowance being stopped if he refused. Another seventy-five-year-old found it so demanding that he cut his own throat.

In 1838-9, the new Guisborough Union erected a workhouse for 130 inmates at the corner of Northgate and Church Lane (NZ614163). In 1894, a forty-eight-bed infirmary was added to the south.

In 1886, a dispute at the workhouse resulted in the resignation or sacking of most of the staff. The Master claimed that the Schoolmistress disobeyed his orders, displayed violent tempers,

A view from around 1905 of Bedale's union workhouse. It could house 100 inmates but by 1921 had an average occupancy of only twenty.

and fostered dissatisfaction amongst the inmates. In turn, the Master, it was claimed, kept thirty or forty hens at the workhouse, and sold the eggs for his own profit. In January 1887, a six-day official enquiry resulted in the Guardians being forced to demand the resignation of the Schoolmistress, the Matron, Master and the porter. In addition, an Assistant Matron and the Head Nurse resigned.

In the 1920s, Tuesday evening dances were held in the workhouse dining-hall which local townsfolk attended. The money raised was used to take children from the union's homes on holiday to Marske or Redcar. The dances ended after one of the Guardians complained that public money was being spent on them, electric light was being used, and the stove was kept on until ten o'clock.

During the Second World War, the former workhouse accommodated military patients from Catterick and Whitby. After 1948 it became Guisborough General and Maternity Hospital and then Guisborough General Hospital. Many of the original workhouse buildings still survive. (TSD)

HELMSLEY

By 1777, local workhouses were in operation at Ampleforth, Helmsley and Kirkby Moorside.

Helmsley Poor Law Union (originally called Helmsley Blackmoor) was created in February 1837. Much of the union was thinly populated bleak moorland owned by men such as Lord Feversham of Dunscombe Park who opposed the 1834 Act. As a result, the union continued to use the small old workhouses at Helmsley and Kirkbymoorside which were said to be 'nurseries of vice and idleness'. The inmates were ill-disciplined and insubordinate and, against regulations, the two Masters performed their duties on a part-time basis, both having other jobs. In 1842, Feversham finally agreed to the building of a new workhouse on Pottergate (SE615838) in Helmsley. However, it accommodated only thirty-five and was badly constructed. By 1846, it had

Easingwold's women inmates performed domestic work and picked oakum, while men did corn-grinding, stone-breaking and gardening. Boys attended a local parish school, but girls were taught reading, writing and needlework by a pauper inmate. The casual wards lacked toilets and beds – vagrants slept on wooden platforms.

Guisborough was a model workhouse. It had water closets (then a novelty) and a slipper bath. It had a piggery, a garden field and a small orchard, and the inmates grew and sold large amounts of potatoes and cabbages. Inmates slept on coconut fibre beds, were regularly shaved, shorn and provided with bibles, prayer books and literature from the SPCK.

Helmsley's High Street workhouse – its predecessor on Pottergate was abandoned after less than thirty years use.

seventeen beds in a cold dark garret occupied by the aged and infirm, both sane and insane, and the mortuary was used by two boys as a bedroom. No work was given to the inmates.

In 1848, because of the difficulties of travel across the union for both guardians and inmates, the union was split into two, with one part forming the new Kirkby Moorside union.

A new Helmsley workhouse was erected in 1859-61 to accommodate sixty-five inmates. It was located on the High Street in Helmsley (SE610839).

The former High Street workhouse building has now been adapted for residential use. (NRY)

KIRKBY MOORSIDE

Kirkbymoorside had a workhouse from 1773 which accommodated twenty inmates.

The area which later formed the Kirkby Moorside Union was originally part of the Helmsley Poor Law Union. However, the size of the Helmsley Union, and remoteness of some of its parts, created difficulties both for guardians and paupers. In 1848, a separate Kirkby Moorside Union was formed and included parishes previously in the Helmsley and Pickering Unions.

In 1850, the new union erected a workhouse for seventy inmates on Gillamoor road in Kirkbymoorside (SE693870). It had a two-storey main block, with smaller single-storey blocks to each side. A small building to the north may have been an infirmary.

The building has now been adapted for residential use. (NRY)

LEYBURN

In 1812-13 Leyburn and five neighbouring townships formed a union under Gilbert's Act. The union had ceased operation by 1834, although at least three poorhouses were still in use, including one in Leyburn – a row of old cottages at the south of Moor Road (SE109906).

In 1837, the new Leyburn Union adopted the old Leyburn poorhouse which could house up to eighty though the average number of inmates was half that. An official inspection in 1866 criticised the comfortless stone flags, the discreditable appearance of the sick wards, and the 'wretched' vagrant wards. There were no water-closets, and the outdoor privies were offensive in warm weather.

A new workhouse was erected in 1875-7 on what is now Quarry Hills Lane (SE115905) to the east of the town. The two-storey main block was constructed in local stone and there was a fifteen-bed infirmary.

The workhouse Master in the 1840s was Robert Warwick, a disabled former naval officer and a man of some notoriety. At various times he was charged with assault, arranging the illegal emigration of paupers to the colonies, and challenging the medical officer to a duel. He also gave vagrants the unpleasant task of pounding limestone into dust for use as fertilizer.

After 1930, the workhouse became a residential home for the elderly and infirm. The building was later used as social services offices but has now been converted to residential use. (NRY)

MALTON

Malton had several early workhouses on a site at Sheepfoot Hill (SE791716). The first, in 1735, was a house known as Spring Hall. In 1789, it was rebuilt to hold 120 paupers. Its treadmill was used both to pump water for the workhouse, and to provide a labour task for the inmates.

In 1837, the new Malton Union took over the Sheepfoot Hill site and extended the buildings to accommodate 160 inmates.

In 1866, an official inspection criticised the ventilation, lighting, water supply, washing facilities and privies. It concluded that a new workhouse was urgently required. This never took place, although in 1893 new male and female infirmaries were added at the east of the site, and a casual ward at the west.

The former Kirkbymoorside workhouse was used in the 1970s to house Vietnamese refugees.

Leyburn's former workhouse at Quarry Hills continued to provide geriatric accommodation until the 1990s.

After 1930, Malton workhouse briefly became a hospital under its original name of Spring Hall but closed in 1934. The casual ward was in use until 1940.

The site is now largely occupied by modern housing. The old male infirmary ward now forms part of a fire station. The old casual ward is occupied by a local pre-school playgroup. (NRY)

MIDDLESBROUGH

Middlesbrough was originally part of the Stockton Poor Law Union. In 1875, following rapid population growth in the area with the development of iron mining, a separate Middlesbrough Union was created.

High unemployment in 1875-6 led to Middlesbrough housing 300 paupers in workhouses of neighbouring unions until its own workhouse was built. Three 'labour test' yards were also set up, providing out-relief in return for manual labour – usually stone-breaking. Unfortunately, the union had trouble disposing of the broken stone and by mid-1879 had over £4,000 worth on its hands.

The new workhouse, for 726 inmates, lay between what is now St Barnabas Road and Ayresome Green Lane (NZ485190). It included a 200-foot-long corridor-plan main building at the south of the site, and a pavilion-plan hospital and school at the centre and north respectively. The first intake of thirteen inmates was admitted on 23 December 1878.

In its early years, the workhouse was frequently criticised. In 1880, a young child was burned to death because there had been no fire screen. In 1882, an 'aged and decrepit female' was found wandering in Stockton after an arbitrary discharge from the workhouse. A year later, three pauper children were found in a Middlesbrough Street by a clergyman after being simply 'put out from the House'. In 1887, after a child drowned in the plunge bath in the Schools block, it was discovered that one or two inmates had sole charge of seventy children in the bath. In 1888, a report on a fever epidemic in the workhouse revealed appalling sanitary arrangements in the main building. As a result, many improvements were undertaken including the building of a new three-storey infirmary and nurses' home, and the erection of a new children's hospital at a separate site (NZ488180).

By 1930, the workhouse had a wireless and there were even cinema shows in the main building.

After 1930, the workhouse main building became Holgate Institution. After 1948, Holgate became an old people's home until 1974 and was then used as an adult training centre. Most of the former workhouse was demolished in the 1980s. The hospital and school portions of the workhouse became the Middlesbrough Municipal Hospital, later Middlesbrough General Hospital. (TSD)

NORTHALLERTON

The former Guildhall near the Sunbeck (SE368941) became Northallerton's first poorhouse in 1730. Inmates were occupied in spinning for the local linen industry. By 1802, workhouses were also in operation at Brompton and Osmotherley.

From its formation in 1837, the Northallerton Union was troubled by local party politics. Guardians from twelve townships in the Whig-dominated Bedale area agitated to have their own union and constantly disrupted proceedings until they finally got their way in March 1839.

Northallerton Union at first retained the Sunbeck workhouse for housing the able-bodied, and the Brompton workhouse for children and the aged. Following the departure of the Bedale Guardians, opposition to the building of a new workhouse increased, and intensified in 1840 with a depression in the linen industry. Brompton workhouse was closed, leaving just the old Northallerton workhouse which held only forty-two inmates. It was described as 'one of the

Northallerton's 1858 workhouse was built on part of Friarage Fields where a medieval Carmelite Friary once stood. The site included the Horse Pond – a former watering stop for stagecoach horses from the busy Great North Road. This view dates from around 1913.

The same scene, barely recognisable, almost ninety years later. Apart from the arrival of the motor vehicle, the workhouse's red-brick walls have been rendered and painted white.

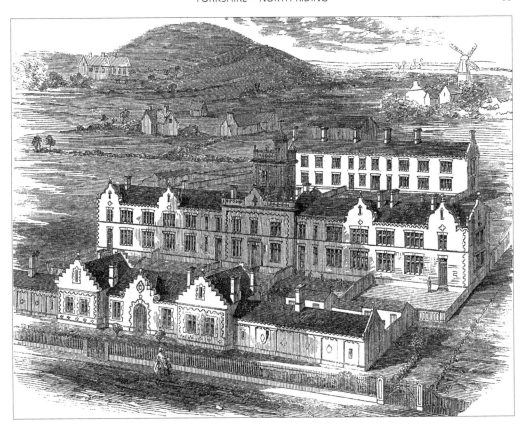

Scarborough's new workhouse on Dean Street (now Dean Road) – on 4 December 1859, the aged paupers were transported here 'by omnibus' from the old Waterhouse Lane premises.

most wretched poorhouses in England', being extremely cramped with small and badly drained yards and a stagnant stream close by. Female inmates 'entertained' men from the streets and inmates sold workhouse property.

A new workhouse for 120 inmates was finally erected in 1857-8 at 'Ware Banks' (SE371942). It was designed by W. Bonython Moffatt, former partner of George Gilbert Scott. The building, echoing Scott and Moffatt's designs from two decades earlier, had a low entrance block with central archway, and a parallel main block behind.

After 1930, the former workhouse became Sunbeck House Public Assistance Institution. During the Second World War, it was first an Emergency Medical Scheme hospital then, from 1943 to 1947, was taken over by RAF Northallerton. In 1948, it became the Friarage Hospital, initially as an orthopaedic hospital for polio victims, then later becoming a general hospital. (NRY)

PICKERING

A poorhouse accommodating thirty inmates existed by 1776 in a street known as 'Under the Cliff' in Pickering. Thornton Dale had a poorhouse from as early as 1734.

After the Pickering Union's formation in January 1837, the Guardians at first planned to retain the existing parish poorhouses with males housed at Pickering, and women and children at Thornton Dale. However, it was soon decided to build a new workhouse for 100 inmates at a site on the Whitby Road at Rysea (SE801844).

Male inmates of the workhouse were employed in breaking whinstone, whilst the women were employed in domestic duties or picked oakum. In 1843, a 'black hole' was erected as a punishment cell for refractory paupers. In 1874, an infirmary wing was added at the east of the workhouse, followed in 1878 by a vagrants' ward.

After 1930, the former workhouse became a children's hospital. An old people's home now occupies the site. (NRY)

REETH

Reeth's original parish workhouse was erected in around 1753 on Back Lane. In the 1770s, it could accommodate fifty inmates.

In 1837, Reeth became part of the new Richmond Poor law Union. However, its remoteness caused travelling problems for paupers, Guardians and the Relieving Officer, particularly in winter. As a result, Reeth and its neighbouring parishes became a separate union in 1840.

A large old house at the south-east of the Market Place (SE039992) was purchased for £700 and converted for use as the Reeth Union workhouse. It accommodated sixty inmates.

Part of the former workhouse building is now a tea-shop and the remainder has reverted to residential use. (NRY)

RICHMOND

In about 1794, Richmond erected a workhouse on Long Hill (NZ166010) at the north-west of the town. The building also incorporated a 'House of Correction' or gaol. The site and the gaol were owned by Richmond Corporation, while the Richmond parish vestry financed the workhouse.

When the Richmond Poor Law Union came into being in February 1837, the shared ownership of the existing workhouse and gaol buildings and site caused some wrangling but in 1839 it was bought by the union for the sum of £1,350. The workhouse was enlarged in 1842 to hold 130 inmates with the erection of vagrant wards and a fever hospital. Later additions included the installation of four water closets in 1847, and a new board-room and vagrants' cell block in 1889.

After 1930, the former workhouse became Richmond House. In 1961, it became a hostel for old people then, in 1968, was converted to an old people's home. The site is now occupied by modern housing. (NRY)

SCARBOROUGH

The first Scarborough workhouse, dating from 1728, was in Waterhouse Lane at the north side of Newborough Street (TA042886).

In 1837, the new Scarborough Union adopted the Waterhouse Lane workhouse and refurbished it to house 170 inmates. However, despite redecoration and new furniture, it was still described as 'an old... straggling, inconvenient building in the centre of the town in a close and bad situation.' In 1842, an adjoining 'house of correction' or prison was converted to provide vagrants' accommodation.

In 1858, a new workhouse for up to 400 inmates was erected on Dean Street (TA039888) and was notable for having mains water and gas lighting.

After 1930, the workhouse became Scarborough Public Assistance Institution. In 1936, twenty beds were added for mental patients. In 1948, the site joined the NHS as St Mary's Hospital which closed in 2000. Only the entrance block now survives. (NRY)

Scarborough's attractive Elizabethan-style entrance block – now the only surviving part of what later became St Mary's Hospital.

Thirsk workhouse gained a reputation as being one of the best managed workhouses in the north, mostly due to the Board of Guardians' vice-chairman Thomas Smith, a local draper and grocer, and a Quaker.

The sloping location of Whitby's workhouse gives it a rather sunken appearance. Before its enlargement in 1860, one directory described it an 'an irregular pile of red bricks'.

STOKESLEY

Stokesley had a parish workhouse for up to fifty inmates on High Green from as early as 1755. Eden's 1797 survey of the poor in England reported of Stokesley that:

> The Poor-house is in good condition. Paupers are taken in at 20d. a week each. Other parishes send their Poor when the house is not full. The master receives the profit of the work done, less a small deduction for each pauper. Table of diet: Breakfast–every day, milk and oatmeal. Dinner–Sunday, beef, roots and dumplins; Monday, hasty pudding, oatmeal; Tuesday, frumenty French barley; Wednesday, beef broth and bread; Thursday, frumenty; Friday, fry and potatoes; Saturday, potatoes and butter and salt fish. Supper–every day, milk and oatmeal. Only one person has died in the house in the last three years.

In 1837, the new Stokesley Union retained the existing parish workhouse but declined to spend any money on adapting it to comply with the 1834 Act. In 1841, Stokesley was described as 'one of the most unbusiness-like unions with one of the most ineffective workhouses'. Eventually, in 1847, the Guardians agreed to build a new workhouse for 104 inmates in Springfield (NZ526089).

The former Stokesley workhouse building is now used as a residential care home. (NRY)

THIRSK

A poorhouse for up to forty paupers was set up in 1737 between Long Street and St James' Green in Thirsk (SE431824). There were also early workhouses at Topcliffe and Sowerby.

In 1838, the new Thirsk Union erected a workhouse for 120 inmates on the north side of Sutton Road in Thirsk (SE434822). Construction of the building provoked anti-Poor Law demonstrations in the town in the summer of 1838 when a mob gathered and effigies were burnt.

Employment for the workhouse's male inmates included stone-breaking and corn-grinding with a hand-mill. Women did domestic work or picked oakum. In 1847, Thirsk was one of the first unions to appoint properly trained teachers.

After 1930, the building stayed empty until pressed into military and first-aid use during the Second World War. It was later used for industrial purposes but in 1998 the infirmary was demolished and the surviving main block was converted to residential use. (NRY)

WHITBY

The first Whitby workhouse, funded by public subscription, was built in 1726-7 on Church Street. In 1794, a new workhouse was erected off Green Lane at the south-east of the town (NZ902105). Being located near the entrance to Boulby's ropery, the site became known as The Ropery. The parish of Ruswarp, at the west of Whitby, had a workhouse which was in use in 1834.

The new Whitby Poor Law Union took over the existing town workhouse in 1837. In 1860, it was enlarged to about twice its size, forming a large U-shape. An entrance block was added at the south, and a school was also erected at the rear of the workhouse.

After 1948, the former workhouse became St Hilda's Hospital and provided geriatric care. St Hilda's closed in 1978 and the surviving buildings are now occupied by small business units. (NRY)

CHAPTER 8
YORKSHIRE – WEST RIDING

Sedbergh

Ripon

Settle

Pateley Bridge

Great Ouseburn

Skipton

Knaresborough

Wharfedale

Wetherby

Keighley

North Bierley

Leeds

Tadcaster

Bradford

Bramley

Selby

Todmorden

Hunslet

Halifax

Dewsbury

Pontefract

Wakefield

Goole

Huddersfield

Hemsworth

Thorne

Saddleworth

Barnsley

Doncaster

Penistone

Wortley

Rotherham

Sheffield

Ecclesall Bierlow

BARNSLEY

Before 1834, Barnsley and Hemsworth shared Ackworth poorhouse (SE439166), built in 1736.

Like a number of other northern industrial areas, Barnsley held out against the formation of a Poor Law Union and its associated central workhouse. The Ackworth workhouse continued in use and, by 1848, was described by an Inspector as being in 'a disgusting state'.

Barnsley Union finally came into being in 1849 and at first employed workhouse premises on St Mary's Place (SE343066), now the site of Barnsley College. Shortly afterwards, a new workhouse was erected on what is now Gawber Road in Barnsley (SE332070).

Life for a seven-year-old in the workhouse in 1911 was later recalled by Thomas Fretwell:

> Friday nights were bath nights. Immediately after tea we were given a good scrub with the brushes the girls used on the floor. No fancy smelling soaps just carbolic and should this get into your eyes it really was painful. Then we were given a flannel nightshirt each. Some reached down to our feet. Some only just covered our knees because they had already been cut down to repair other night-shirts. Then we were lined up in front of the Matron who gave us a dose of brimstone and treacle then off to bed. We used to tie our clothes up with the jacket sleeves and shove them under the bed.

After 1930, the site became St Helen's Hospital. A major reconstruction of the hospital has resulted in the demolition of the workhouse buildings. (BAR)

BARWICK-IN-ELMET

In 1825, forty parishes to the north and east of Leeds formed a Gilbert Union based at Barwick-in-Elmet. A small union workhouse – a row of cottages – was situated at Barwick (SE391373).

Because of its Gilbert Union status, Barwick-in-Elmet was largely exempt from the provisions of the 1834 Poor Law Act. However, because its member parishes were so scattered, the PLC tried, unsuccessfully, to persuade Barwick-in-Elmet and the other Gilbert Unions in the area (Great Ouseburn, Carlton, and Great Preston) to reconstitute as Poor Law Unions.

The union survived until 1869 when all remaining Gilbert Unions were abolished. Many of its member parishes and townships joined the new Tadcaster Union created in 1862. (YWL)

BRADFORD

In the 1770s, workhouses were in operation at Bradford, Allerton, Calverley with Farsley, Clayton, Heaton, Horton, Idle, Manningham, North Bierley and Bowling, and Thornton.

Following the creation of the Bradford Poor Law Union in February 1837, the town was the scene of vigorous anti-Poor Law campaigning. This peaked in October during a visit of Assistant Commissioner Alfred Power – his meetings with the Guardians were disrupted and he was attacked by a crowd. A contingent of six London police officers was sent to maintain order. Eventually, cavalry troops from Leeds were called in to quell a mob attacking a meeting at the Courthouse.

Bradford continued to resist the building of a new workhouse. It retained old premises at the south side of what is now Barkerend Road (SE172334), and a property at Idle (SE171387) which an 1847 directory noted 'has twice been enlarged for the use of Bradford Union'.

Eventually, the Guardians relented and in 1849-52 erected a large new workhouse and infirmary for 350 inmates on a 14-acre site at Little Horton Lane (SE158320) at a total cost of £11,000.

The new workhouse had problems with its staff – the Master in 1851 was suspended for habitual drunkenness and immoral conduct. In 1852, the Guardians demanded the resignations

The main building of Bradford's Little Horton workhouse, now the site of St Luke's Hospital.

The main block of Bramley workhouse had the Master and Matron's quarters at its centre, with females accommodated to the right and males to the left. A porter's lodge, receiving wards, offices and the board-room lay near the entrance at the north of the site.

of the Master and Matron for incompetence, and the workhouse tailor was dismissed for 'an improper connection with a young female inmate'.

The former workhouse site at Little Horton is now the home of St Luke's Hospital.

In 1910, Bradford erected a 'labour test' workhouse solely for able-bodies inmates at Daisy Hill (SE129349). The site is now Lynfield Mount Hospital and provides psychiatric care.

The union also built a TB sanatorium at Eastby (SE025550). (YWB)

BRAMLEY

By 1777, local workhouses existed at Armley, Farnley, Gildersome and Wortley.

The Bramley Poor Law Union was created in 1862 to serve the west of Leeds and Pudsey. It comprised the parishes of Armley, Bramley, Farnley, Gildersome and Wortley. In 1871-2, the union erected a new workhouse for 220 inmates on Green Hill Road in Armley (SE256338). The total cost was £15,500 and the architects were C.S. and A.J. Nelson who also designed the Wharfedale Union workhouse at Otley.

The former workhouse later became St Mary's Hospital, providing care for the elderly. (YWL)

CARLTON

In October 1818, seventeen Wharfedale parishes and townships formed a large Gilbert Union based at East Carlton, two miles to the south of Otley. A further fourteen members joined in 1819, six more in 1824, and three more in 1826. The union had a workhouse at East Carlton (SE221431) and also used a building on Cross Green in Otley (SE206457).

Its Gilbert Union status largely exempted Carlton from the provisions of the 1834 Act. However, because its member parishes were so scattered, the PLC tried, unsuccessfully, to persuade Carlton and other Gilbert Unions in the area to convert to Poor Law Unions.

In 1861, a new Wharfedale Union was created, and was joined by many former Carlton Union parishes. The Carlton Union was abolished in 1869 along with the other remaining Gilbert Unions. (YWW)

DEWSBURY

Early workhouses existed at Dewsbury, Batley, Gomersal, Heckmondwike, Liversedge, Mirfield and Ossett. Dewsbury's workhouse was a converted farm at Balk Hill (SE232214).

After Dewsbury Union was set up in February 1837, the town saw an upsurge of anti-Poor Law protest. Opposition candidates dominated the Guardians' elections in March 1838, and the new Board resolved not to implement the 1834 Act. The PLC tried, without success, to get the Board's pro-Poor Law vice-chairman Joshua Ingham and other ex officio guardians to carry out the law. In August 1838, an open meeting of the Guardians was halted when the audience became violent, and troops were summoned from Leeds. For the next meeting, 100 Lancers, 76 riflemen, 200 Metropolitan Police and 600 special constables were present to keep order.

The Guardians continued using old township workhouses at Balk Hill, Gomersal (SE214259) and Batley (SE223250). An 1854 official inspection found that the union was disobeying a number of regulations, for example that married inmates should be separated, and that workhouse uniforms be worn. Later that year, the union finally agreed to build a new workhouse at Staincliffe (SE233228). In the 1880s, a large pavilion-plan infirmary was erected south of the workhouse.

After 1930, the former workhouse was renamed Batley Institution, with the hospital facilities becoming Staincliffe Hospital. The Institution mainly accommodated the elderly and was renamed Beech Towers in 1950. The former workhouse buildings have now all been replaced. (YWK)

Inmates posed in front of Doncaster's Hexthorpe Lane workhouse in the 1890s. The porter (left) is carrying a small dog.

A decade or so later, the Doncaster workhouse officers and staff are pictured at the new premises at Springwell Lane.

DONCASTER

In 1719, the Doncaster Corporation and local gentry provided £558 to purchase 'a workhouse or a house of maintenance, to get the poor of this town to work, who have become very numerous.' This opened in about 1730, near what is now Pell Close (SE574031). There were also early workhouses at Bawtry, Barnby Dun and Tickhill.

In 1837, the new Doncaster Board of Guardians purchased a site in Hexthorpe (SE570027) on which to erect a union workhouse. Unfortunately, it was very close to Great Northern Railway's new engineering works which produced much industrial smoke, noise and vibration. Eventually, the Guardians decided to erect new premises at Springwell Lane, Balby. In 1901, the old site was sold to the GNR and the buildings were used for storage until being demolished in the late 1960s.

One Hexthorpe inmate in 1871 was John Broxholme, abandoned as a three-year-old on Broxholme Lane in 1862. The supposed parents were traced to Sheffield but found to be unmarried and penniless. The child was thus taken unto the workhouse under the name 'John Broxholme'.

The new Springwell Lane workhouse (SE556005), for up to 600 inmates, was erected in 1897-1900 at a cost of £70,000. Its pavilion-block design featured a central administrative building connected by corridors to separate blocks for the different classes of inmate. At its opening, the Chairman of the Guardians pronounced the buildings to be the most up-to-date in England and that their fame had spread so far that the Emperor and Empress of Russia had asked for the plans so as to build a similar establishment in their own country.

After 1930, the site was renamed Springwell House Public Assistance Institution, then in 1950 became Western Hospital, mostly caring for maternity and geriatric patients. It was demolished in 1974 and the site redeveloped for a primary school and private housing. (DON)

ECCLESALL BIERLOW

In 1777, workhouses were in use at Ecclesall Bierlow, Nether Hallam, Dore and Norton.

The Ecclesall Bierlow Union, formed in 1837, covered the area to the west of Sheffield. The union originally planned to use an existing workhouse on Psalter Lane at Sharrow Moor, but the building could not easily be enlarged. In 1844, a new workhouse was opened on Cherry Tree Lane (later Union Road) at Nether Edge (SK337849).

The site was later renamed Ecclesall Institution, then after 1929 became Nether Edge Hospital. As well as general wards it included tuberculosis sanatoria and a maternity hospital. In 1940, bombing destroyed several buildings including the dining hall and nurses' home. The hospital closed in the 1990s and the site has now been redeveloped for residential use.

In 1903, the union set up a cottage homes site at Fulwood (SK294857). (SHE)

GOOLE

Goole Poor Law Union was formed in October 1837. In 1839, the union erected a workhouse on Booth Ferry Road in Goole (SE742239). It was designed by John and William Atkinson, the architects of many other Yorkshire workhouses including those at Bedale, Beverley, Easingwold, Guisborough, Helmsley, Howden, Kirkby Moorside, Pateley Bridge, Pocklington, Skirlaugh, Wetherby and York. Their design for Goole was unusual, with the various inmates' quarters closely arranged around a small central courtyard as opposed to the more popular cruciform or hexagonal layouts. Later additions included an infirmary and fever hospital at the north, and a casual ward at the east.

After 1930, Goole workhouse became Goole Poor Law Institution and later St John's Hospital. The buildings have now been demolished and the site is now occupied by a supermarket. (YER)

The E-shaped main block of the Ecclesall Bierlow workhouse, roofless prior to the building's renovation in 2001.

This unusual early 1900s view shows the view *from* the main block of the Ecclesall Bierlow workhouse. The building opposite originally housed the union's offices but was later used as a school.

In the 1930s, the former Great Ouseburn workhouse was used for local cinema shows. During the Second World War it was an anti-aircraft station and also housed Italian prisoners of war, guarded by a Scottish regiment. Prisoners were escorted to Sunday church services in the nearby village accompanied by bagpipes.

An early view of the Hemsworth workhouse and its new infirmary (left). Some of the workhouse inmates can be seen at the centre of the picture.

GREAT OUSEBURN

In 1828, forty parishes to the west of York formed the Great Ouseburn Gilbert Union which erected a workhouse near Great Ouseburn (SE435618).

Its Gilbert Union status exempted Great Ouseburn from most of the provisions of the 1834 Poor Law Act. However, in 1853, the PLC used a legal technicality to forcibly dissolve the Gilbert Union and create a new Poor Law Union in its place. The new union erected a workhouse on the site of the old building. Designed by J. & W. Atkinson of York, it could accommodate sixty inmates.

In 1930, the site was taken over by the West Riding County Council who found conditions primitive. Water was drawn from wells, heating was mostly by open fires, and electricity came from a paraffin engine. As a result, the establishment was closed down. In 1953, the buildings were acquired by seed merchants Campbell & Penty. (YNR)

GREAT PRESTON

In July 1809, twenty parishes and townships to the south and east of Leeds joined to form the Great Preston Gilbert Union. Successive additions eventually took the membership to forty-one places. The union's workhouse was the former Great Preston Hall (SE402297).

Its Gilbert Union status exempted Great Preston from most of the provisions of the 1834 Poor Law Act. However, because its member parishes were so scattered, the PLC tried, unsuccessfully, to persuade Great Preston and the three other Gilbert Unions in the area (Great Ouseburn, Barwick-in-Elmet, and Carlton) to convert to Poor Law Unions.

Great Preston survived until 1869 when all remaining Gilbert Unions were abolished. Its member parishes were then distributed among the Poor Law Unions in the area. (NON)

HALIFAX

In 1635, Charles I granted Halifax a charter to set up a workhouse. The town was given a large house for the purpose by Nathaniel Waterhouse. By 1797, the workhouse accommodated eighty-nine paupers and was said to be 'small and inconvenient'.

In 1838, the new Halifax Union's Board of Guardians reviewed the fourteen workhouses they had inherited which were located at: Halifax, Southowram, Hipperholme cum Brighouse, Northowram, Rastrick, Elland cum Greetland, Stainland, Warley, Soyland, Sowerby, Shelf, Ovenden, Skircoat and Norland. Some were said to be 'in a state unfit for human beings to inhabit'. The Board decided to erect a new workhouse on land between Gibbet Lane and Hanson Lane (SE083253).

The new building adopted the popular cruciform layout with four wings radiating from an octagonal hub. In 1869, two large three-storey infirmary pavilions were erected behind the workhouse at a cost of £30,000 – they were said to be 'the last word' in hospital construction. In 1872 a large dining-hall cum chapel was built.

The workhouse site later became known as St John's Public Assistance Institution, and was used as an old people's home until 1949. The buildings no longer exist.

In 1901, the union also opened a large infirmary at Salterhebble (SE096232). The site later operated as St Luke's Hospital and, after 1948, as Halifax General Hospital. (YWC)

HEMSWORTH

Before 1834, Barnsley and Hemsworth shared Ackworth poorhouse (SE439166), built in 1736.

Hemsworth was one of the areas in the West Riding which caused problems for the PLC. A legacy of Gilbert Unions and independent townships, coupled with a general economic depression in the 1840s, delayed progress in unionisation. Eventually, the old Ackworth workhouse was condemned after an inspector found it to be in 'a disgusting condition'.

The new Hemsworth Poor Law Union was created in 1850, and a new workhouse was finally built in 1859 on Southmoor Road (SE429126). Its design used the cruciform layout popular in the 1830s. Later additions included a Guardians' board-room in 1895, casual wards in 1900, an infirmary in 1903, a Master's house in about 1920, and a further infirmary block in 1923.

In 1930, the workhouse became a Public Assistance Institution providing accommodation for the elderly. Electricity was installed throughout the site in 1935 – prior to then lighting had been by gas with the exception of the porter's lodge, board-room and Master's house.

The site later became Southmoor Hospital. The Master's house and 1903 infirmary survive. (YWW)

HOLBECK

In the 1770s, Holbeck had a workhouse with accommodation for up to forty-five inmates.

From 1844 to 1862, Holbeck, at the west of Leeds, was under the jurisdiction of the Leeds Guardians. Then, because of population growth in the area, Holbeck became an independent Poor Law Parish. In 1869, following the abolition of the Carlton Gilbert Union, a Holbeck Poor Law Union was formed covering Holbeck, Beeston and Churwell. The union operated until 1904 when Holbeck reverted to being an independent Poor Law Parish.

In 1863-4 a new Holbeck workhouse was erected at the south of Elland Road (SE295319). Designed by William Hill of Leeds, its construction cost over £6,000. The building had a T-shaped main block with males accommodated at one side and females at the other. In 1881-3, the main block was enlarged and a new 100-bed infirmary added at the east of the site. Further additions in 1903 included new receiving wards, laundry, kitchens and bakery.

After 1930, the site provided accommodation for the elderly and homeless – a sign over the entrance read 'Home for Destitute People'. The workhouse buildings no longer exist. (YWL)

HUDDERSFIELD

In the 1770s, workhouses were in use at Huddersfield, Aldmonbury, Kirkheaton and Lockwood. Township workhouses also existed at Honley, Lepton, Golcar, Linthwaite, Marsden, Wooldale, Thurstonland, Slaithwaite, Upperthong and Lindley.

The Huddersfield Poor Law Union was formed in February 1837. Strong anti-Poor Law feeling in the area was led by Richard Oastler, veteran of the 'Ten Hour Bill' campaign for better factory conditions. The first Board of Guardians had a majority of anti-Poor Law members and refused to appoint a Clerk, without which the business of the union could not proceed. Its early meetings were turbulent with and frequently disrupted by angry, and sometimes violent, crowds. The Poor Law Commissioners eventually threatened to dissolve the union and also applied pressure on local magistrates (who were ex officio members of the Board). At the end of January 1838, a Clerk was finally appointed. However, resistance continued by other means.

The Board declined to build a new workhouse but decided to retain the five largest township workhouses at: Huddersfield (SE138177), Almondbury (SE162147), Kirkheaton (SE181185), Golcar (SE085161) and Honley (SE137118), and to close the other smaller ones. The scheme provoked opposition in the townships where the smaller workhouses were located and some appear to have continued in operation.

The old buildings were often little more than converted houses. The Huddersfield township workhouse was particularly unsuited. From 1843 onwards, complaints about its facilities for treatment of the sick were regularly made by union medical officer, Thomas Tatham. Eventually, in 1848, an official inquiry uncovered appalling conditions:

> ...the sick poor have been most shamefully neglected... patients have been allowed to remain for nine weeks together without a change of linen or of bed clothing: that beds in which patients suffering in typhus have died, have been repeatedly used for fresh patients, without any change or attempt at purification; that the said beds were only bags of straw and shavings, for the most part laid on the floor, and that the whole swarmed with lice; that two patients suffering in infectious fever, were almost constantly put together in one bed, that it not unfrequently happened that one would be ragingly delirious, when the other was dying.

A second report found further horrors – forty children were found occupying a room 24 feet by 15 feet and sleeping up to ten in a bed, while fifty adult males fitted into a room 23 feet by 18 feet.

Despite the resulting outcry, things were slow to change. The old buildings were eventually replaced by new workhouses at Deanhouse in 1862, and at Crosland Moor in 1871. The old town workhouse became an infectious diseases hospital known as Birkby Hospital.

The Deanhouse workhouse (SE137099) was at Netherthong to the south of Huddersfield. Designed by John Kirk, it had a two-storey T-shaped main block. A pavilion-plan infirmary was added in 1880. The buildings have now been demolished and the site redeveloped for housing.

The Crosland Moor workhouse (SE126154), also by Kirk, was on Barton Road (now Blackmoorfoot Road) at the south-west of Huddersfield. The site later became St Luke's Hospital. Many original buildings still exist. (YWK)

HUNSLET

Hunslet's earliest workhouse was in Carr Hall, a house on Hunslet Moor side, which was hired for the purpose. A new township workhouse was erected in 1760 on Hillidge Road (SE306317).

The fine Gothic-style main building of Huddersfield's Crosland Moor workhouse was three storeys high, over 200 feet long, and constructed of local stone. The central tower held a large tank containing 10,000 gallons of water. There were also separate hospital and school buildings.

Hunslet's Rothwell Haigh site, officially opened in October 1903, was one of the last new workhouses ever built. It comprised entrance buildings, main building, laundry and boiler house, infirmary, lunacy block and isolation hospital. It was lit throughout by electricity – there were 1,130 lamps, and also nineteen telephones in the buildings.

The entrance to Keighley workhouse – at the left were the board-room, Master's office and receiving wards. A porter's lodge and male vagrants' block were erected to the right of the entrance in 1887. The vagrants' work cells contained corn-grinding devices which required 8,800 turns to grind four bushels (145 litres) of corn.

A barred enclosure in Keighley's workhouse cellars may have been used as a 'refractory cell' for inmates who broke workhouse rules.

The magnificent Starbeck Hall, which was erected as Harrogate's workhouse in 1810, then was briefly used by the new Knaresborough Union.

After 1834, Hunslet continued as an independent township, still using the Hillidge Road workhouse. In June 1869, the new Hunslet Poor Law Union was created. Hillidge Road was enlarged by the addition of a separate infirmary in 1867, and school buildings in 1872.

In 1900, work began on a new workhouse and infirmary at Rothwell Haigh (SE330290). The new buildings were planned to hold 450 inmates.

In 1934, the site became St George's Hospital and was used for the chronic sick. The hospital finally closed in December 1991. The workhouse buildings no longer exist.

The union also erected a row of cottage homes on Wood Lane, Rothwell (SE335290), a few hundred yards east of the workhouse. (YWL)

KEIGHLEY

In the 1770s, local workhouses were in operation at Keighley, Bingley and Haworth.

Like many of its neighbours, the Keighley Union, formed in 1837, resisted the construction of a central workhouse, preferring to provide a 'dole' during periods of recession. Old workhouses continued in use at Exley Head (SE048400) to the south of Keighley, and on Myrtle Place at Bingley (SE107390).

A new union workhouse was finally erected in 1858 at the north side of Oakworth road in Keighley (SE055408). The main building provided male accommodation at the east, and female at the west. The dining hall stood to the rear.

In 1930, the former workhouse was renamed Keighley Public Assistance Institution. It later became Hillworth Lodge old people's home and was afterwards used by Keighley College. In 2000, the site was refurbished for residential use.

Keighley also set up cottage homes on Nashville Road (SE054407) and an infirmary on Fell Lane (SE049406) (KEI)

KNARESBOROUGH

In 1737, Knaresborough set up a parish workhouse next to the church – the inmates wove flax. Allerton, Brearton and Dacre shared a workhouse on the Green at Scriven. Bilton and Harrogate used a workhouse at Land Green Farm at Pannal. Harrogate erected its own workhouse at Starbeck, now a listed building known as Starbeck Hall (SE327559).

The unionization of West Yorkshire was severely hindered by the continuing existence of four Gilbert Unions (Barwick, Carlton, Great Ouseburn and Great Preston). This began to change in the 1850s with the formation of several new unions including Knaresborough in 1854.

Initially, the union continued using the workhouse at Starbeck. A new workhouse, designed by Isaac Shutt of Harrogate, was built in 1857 on Stockwell Road in Knaresborough (SE351573).

After 1930, the site continued providing care for the elderly, with remaining orphan children being moved to a children's home in Scriven. The vagrants' wards continued in use until 1950. After 1948, the site became Knaresborough Hospital but was demolished in 1996. (YNR)

LEEDS

The first Leeds workhouse opened in 1638 in Lady Lane and was re-established there in 1726. In 1740 a workroom, granary, washhouse, brewhouse and infirmary were added, followed by lunatic cells in 1771. In 1797, Eden reported of Leeds that:

There are 154 inmates in the Workhouse, of whom 42 are old and infirm men or lunatics, 56 women, many of them soldiers' wives, and 56 children mostly under 12. There are a few cripples or idiots between 12 and 20. Children are generally bound apprentices at 9 or 10. The Workhouse is an old building, in the town, with accommodation for 200 persons. There are about 20 beds in each room, chiefly of flocks and provided each with 2 blankets and a rug. Some beds have sheets.

Leeds at first adopted a policy of non-cooperation with the New Poor Law. However, on 21 November 1844, this changed when the PLC placed the township's poor relief administration under the control of a body called the Leeds Guardians.

In 1846-8, the Guardians erected the 'Moral and Industrial Training Schools' – a workhouse for children – on the north side of Beckett Street in Leeds (SE317347). In 1858-61, a new workhouse was built alongside. The buildings comprised a large T-shaped main block, infirmary and chapel. 'Idiotic' wards were added in 1863, followed by another infirmary in 1874, a nurses' home in 1894, and a ward for 'imbeciles' in 1900.

The workhouse buildings later became part of St James' Hospital but now house the Thackray Medical Museum.

In 1901, the Guardians erected a central home for their scattered homes scheme on Street Lane (SE321388). (YWL)

NORTH BIERLEY

A rapid growth in the population of the Bradford Union led, in 1848, to the creation of the new North Bierley Union from a group of suburban parishes and townships around Bradford.

The new union erected a workhouse in 1855-8 at Clayton (SE124311). The building, for 400 inmates, was designed by Lockwood & Mawson, architects of union workhouses at Bradford, Barnsley, Kingston-upon-Hull, Dewsbury and Penistone.

After 1930, the site was developed as a hospital. In 1948, it became part of the NHS and renamed Thornton View. The site is now a school and many original buildings still exist. (KEI)

PATELEY BRIDGE

Pateley Bridge had a small workhouse to the east of the town above the Knott (SE171655).

The Pateley Bridge Union was formed in February 1837. The new union resisted the building of a new central workhouse, preferring parishes to make local arrangements or obtain pauper accommodation on contract as required, e.g. children were sent to the Leeds Moral and Industrial School. The old Knott workhouse continued in operation.

A new union workhouse was eventually erected in 1862-3 near St Cuthbert's Church (SE158658). It received its first occupants in November 1863. The Master and Matron were John Thompson and his wife Elizabeth who received salaries of £18 and £12 per annum respectively.

The workhouse closed in 1914, after the Guardians refused to pay for improvements demanded by the Local Government Board. Existing inmates were transferred to Ripon workhouse.

The building was later used as offices by the Water Board and local council. Part of the site is now occupied by the Nidderdale Museum. (YNR)

PENISTONE

Penistone Poor Law Union was formed in July 1849 from eight parishes or townships formerly in the Wortley Union, and seven others not previously part of any union.

The union built a new workhouse in 1859 on Huddersfield Road, Penistone (SE244039). An infirmary was erected at the north-east of the workhouse in 1895.

During the First World War, the buildings housed convalescent wounded soldiers. In 1928, the workhouse suffered an outbreak of smallpox, probably introduced by vagrants from Barnsley.

Leeds new workhouse was opened on 28 March 1861. It could accommodate 800 inmates. In 1915, the site was taken over by the military and became the East Leeds War Hospital.

North Bierley's workhouse was located adjacent to the Horton Bank reservoir. It had a two-storey entrance building with a central archway and a casual block at its southern end. The three-storey T-shaped main building accommodated females at the north and males at the south. The central wing at the rear contained the dining-hall and kitchens.

During the First World War, the Pateley Bridge workhouse housed German prisoners of war. After the war, it accommodated workers on the Scar Dam project. The casual wards remained in use until around 1939, providing vagrants with a staging post between Ripon and Skipton.

In 1930, the site became a Public Assistance Institution, then from 1948 to 1974 was Netherfield Aged Persons Home. The buildings now house Penistone Grammar School's sixth-form college. (SHE)

PONTEFRACT

Pontefract had a poorhouse called Bead House which closed in 1811, and also a large workhouse site on Micklegate (SE460222). The town was part of the Great Preston Gilbert Union, formed in 1809.

Pontefract Poor Law Union was created in 1862 and included other former members of the Great Preston Union. The new union erected a workhouse in 1862-4 at the north of Pontefract between Skinner Lane and Back Northgate (SE457223). It had a three-storey main building, a large infirmary, and a separate block for mothers and children.

In 1930, the site became Headlands Public Assistance Institution, accommodating mainly the elderly. Electricity was installed in 1935. In 1938, the building was used for gas-mask training. In 1948, the site became Northgate Lodge Hospital but has now been completely redeveloped with only the main workhouse block still surviving. (YWW)

RIPON

Ripon had two seventeenth-century workhouses – one at Sharow, the other within the Archbishop's manor-house where the court house now stands. In 1777, Allhallowgate Hall was given by John Aislabie for use as a workhouse.

As in many other northern areas, Ripon resisted the 1834 Poor Law Act and refused to co-operate with the PLC. Ripon Poor Law Union was finally formed in 1852 and erected a new workhouse on the existing Allhallowgate site (SE313715). The architects were Perkin & Backhouse who also designed Armley Gaol in Leeds.

In 1930, the workhouse became a Public Assistance Institution. In 1948, the main buildings became Sharow View old people's home. The casual wards, or 'Wayfarers' Reception Centre', closed in around 1960.

The main building now houses social services offices. The old workhouse buildings are home to Ripon Workhouse Museum and provide a vivid insight into the former life of the establishment. (YNR)

ROTHERHAM

Rotherham's 'Cottage Workhouse' was set up on The Crofts in 1659. It was run by a local body called the Feoffees. Workhouses also existed at Rawmarsh and Laughton.

The Rotherham Poor Law Union, formed in July 1837, paid the Feoffees £1,000 for a 5-acre site south of Alma Road (SK431922) on which to build a new workhouse. It opened in July 1840 and could accommodate 300 inmates.

A Poor Law Board inspection in 1867 recorded that the inmates included 140 old and infirm, and about sixty children. There was only one nurse for 140 patients, conditions in the sick wards were poor, and the sanitation was defective. Following an outbreak of smallpox in Rotherham in 1872, the workhouse was used for isolation purposes and out of 141 people admitted, twenty-two died. In 1894, a major rebuilding of the workhouse took place.

After 1930, the workhouse became Alma Road Public Assistance Institution, then Moorgate General Hospital. The hospital closed in around 1980 and was demolished in the late 1980s.

In 1910, the union established a sanatorium at Badsley Moor (SK445928). (ROT)

The main building of Penistone's 1859 workhouse had a cruciform layout with an octagonal hub, harking back to the radial designs popular in the 1830s. Males were placed at the west, and females at the east, with a dining hall and kitchen to the rear.

Ripon's Allhallowgate workhouse – now the home of the Ripon Workhouse Museum. The entrance block had an archway at the centre, side-wings containing receiving wards for new inmates, and casual wards to the rear. The T-shaped main building included the Master's house at the front, and the inmates' dining hall behind.

An early 1900s view of the Sedbergh workhouse which could accommodate up to sixty-five inmates. The buildings comprised a T-shaped main building, together with a porter's lodge and casual ward block.

SADDLEWORTH

The Saddleworth with Quick Gilbert Union operated from around 1810 until 1853. The union used a workhouse on Running Hill Lane near Dobcross (SE007069). An old poorhouse also existed on Knarr Barn Lane, Delph (SD978071).

In May 1853, the union was dissolved and Saddleworth became a Poor Law Parish under the 1834 Poor Law Act. The parish carried on using the old workhouse on Running Hill Lane which was enlarged in 1855.

In 1894, Saddleworth formed a Poor Law Union with the parishes of Springhead and Upper Mill, with the union taking over the Running Hill Lane site.

In 1930, the site passed to the West Riding County Council. At that time, it accommodated about eighty inmates, was lit by gas, and was supplied with water from an adjoining private reservoir, although the water was not filtered in any way. It is believed that the building continued in use for a few years as a geriatric hospital. (NON)

SEDBERGH

In the 1770s, a local workhouse was in operation at 'Sedberg' for up to thirty inmates. In 1789, the Sedbergh's poor were 'let' to a contractor at an annual fee of £195. A house near Settlbeck was used first, then a building on Main Street opposite the foot of New Street (SD660921).

Sedbergh Poor Law Union was created in January 1840. It was the smallest union in the West Riding of Yorkshire, comprising only three parishes: Sedbergh, Garsdale and Dent. Initially, the union continued using old workhouses at Sedbergh, which could house fifty-five inmates, and at Hall Bank to the north-east of Dent (SD712873), which held forty-five.

A new Sedbergh Union workhouse for sixty inmates was eventually erected in 1857 at the south of Sedbergh on the road to Dent (SD659917).

After 1930, the site was used for some years as a home for the elderly. The buildings have now been converted to residential use. (CUK)

SELBY

A 1777 parliamentary report listed a workhouse at Selby for up to twenty inmates.

Selby Poor Law Union was formed in February 1837 and erected a workhouse later the same year at a site on Union Lane in Selby (SE611320). The main building lay at the east of the site with a porter's lodge to its east. A casuals' block ran along the roadside at the south of the site with Guardians' board-room at its west, both of these blocks dating from 1891.

After 1930, the former workhouse became a Public Assistance Institution.

The site is now occupied by a home and day centre for the elderly. The former board-room and casual-ward block, now much altered, still survive. (NRY)

SETTLE

Settle had a workhouse from at least 1738. Then, in 1759, 'two dwelling-houses, a barn, and two gardens in Upper Settle' were leased for use as a 'convenient poor-house sufficient to hold all the poor belonging to the said township of Settle'. Nearby Giggleswick was part of a Gilbert Union of seven parishes which, in 1834, erected a poorhouse on Raines Road at Giggleswick (SD810638).

The new Settle Poor Law Union, formed in January 1837, took over and enlarged the Giggleswick workhouse. Later additions included a hospital block, a block for mental defectives at the south of the workhouse, and casual wards at the north of the site.

In the 1930s, the site was used as a mental deficiency colony. In 1948, it became Castleberg Hospital, providing care for the elderly and those with learning difficulties. Some of the buildings have now been converted to residential use. (NRY)

The Settle Union workhouse at Giggleswick – undergoing conversion to housing in 2001.

SHEFFIELD

Sheffield Corporation erected a workhouse in around 1628. By the 1770s, workhouses were operating at Sheffield, Attercliffe with Darnall, and Brightside Bierlow.

Sheffield Poor Law Union was created in June 1837. It took over an existing workhouse on Kelham Street (SK353880), converted in 1829 from a cotton mill to house 600 inmates. Brightside Township workhouse at Pitsmoor (SK356885) was also kept for use by children. In the 1840s, the union had an ancillary workhouse at Hollow Meadows (SK256879) where inmates cleared and cultivated 50 acres of moorland.

Kelham Street became increasingly overcrowded and had no provision for the sick. In 1856, plans began for a move to a new site. However, the scheme was delayed for almost twenty years by opposition from local ratepayers. Finally, in 1874, the Board acquired a 44-acre site at Fir Vale (SK362907) for a large new workhouse. When it opened in 1880, the total cost was a massive £180,000. The buildings included a main block for 1,800 inmates, an asylum for 200, a school building for 200 children, a hospital for 366 patients, a fever hospital, and vagrants' wards.

In 1896, Mr Pye-Smith, a local surgeon, recorded a visit to the workhouse:

> In the sewing room, where some 60 or more old women were busily engaged making the same ugly garments that they are forced to wear. Passing through one of the day-rooms, where a few books seemed to be the only source of recreation, we came to the Nursery, where in their quaint little cage-like cradles, infants were being attended by infirm old women. How unlike the bright young nursemaids one sees in ordinary life! We have recently been told why the babies are considerably removed from such influences when they arrive at three years of age!

In 1894, the union pioneered the use of scattered homes and a headquarters home was erected at the south of the workhouse.

The main building of Sheffield's Fir Vale workhouse. Work for able-bodied inmates included cutting firewood, of which about five tons were sold weekly. Each week, the laundry washed about 20,000 articles, and the bread store cut up 2,600 loaves.

In 1815, Sheffield was one of several urban workhouses at the time to issue poor relief in the form of specially minted tokens which could be used at local shops and then redeemed by shop-keepers.

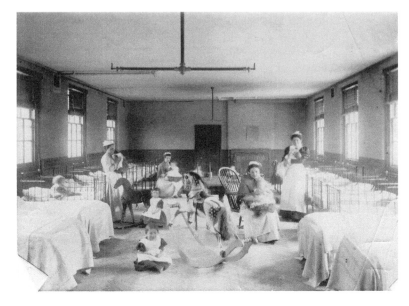

The nursery at the Fir Vale workhouse, c.1902. Only six years after Mr Pye-Smith's visit, the children now appear to being cared for by some 'bright young nursemaids'. The room is also fitted with Venetian blinds and parquet flooring.

Skipton had a reputation as more humane than many other workhouses. In 1852, local man Benson Bailey wrote of the 'cleanliness, comfort and cheerfulness' of the inmates. The elderly received a tobacco allowance, and in 1871 the workhouse children had an excursion to Morecambe.

In 1906, the hospital separated under the name Sheffield Union Hospital, but gradually became known as Fir Vale Hospital. After 1930, the workhouse became Fir Vale Infirmary, while the hospital became City General Hospital. After 1948, the whole site became the City General Hospital, then in 1967 was renamed the Northern General. Some original buildings still survive. (SHE)

SKIPTON

In the 1770s, there were workhouses in use at Skipton, Grassington and Kettlewell.

The new Skipton Poor Law Union, formed in January 1837, erected a workhouse for 200 inmates in 1838-40 on Gargrave Road in Skipton (SD985520). It had an unusual H-shaped layout. The front part of the main block contained the board-room and offices at the centre, with males housed at the west and females at the east. The central section to the rear contained dining-hall, kitchens and the Master's quarters, while the rear wing was used for infirm and children's accommodation. Later additions included a forty-eight-bed infirmary and vagrants' block.

In 1930, the workhouse became a Public Assistance Institution, and the children transferred to the nearby County Children's Home. The site later became Raikeswood Hospital which closed in around 1990. The surviving buildings have now been converted to residential use. (NRY)

TADCASTER

Until the 1860s, East and West Tadcaster had separate arrangements for poor relief. From 1826, East Tadcaster was part of the Barwick-in-Elmet Gilbert Union and used the union's

A survey of Thorne workhouse in 1930, by its new owners the West Riding County Council, noted that the establishment was scrupulously clean but heated by open fires and lit by gas. Too small to become a Public Assistance Institution, it was closed a few years later. The casual wards stayed open until 1941.

An aerial view of the Wakefield workhouse site from the west – the main workhouse buildings are at the left. To the right is the 150-bed pavilion-plan infirmary erected in 1898. Its advanced facilities included filtered, washed and humidified air, electric lighting, and its own telephone system. During the First World War, it provided 100 beds for military patients.

workhouse at Barwick. West Tadcaster operated its own workhouse in a house on St Joseph Street (SE484433).

Eventually, in 1862, a new Tadcaster Union was created although its members originally included only West Tadcaster whose workhouse was adopted by the new union.

In February 1865, the West Tadcaster workhouse was the subject of scandal which came to light after the funeral of pauper Elizabeth Daniel. Her body was taken to the churchyard on a chimney sweep's donkey cart followed by a horse-drawn cart carrying an effigy of the workhouse Matron, Mrs Levers, which was later burnt on a bonfire. The procession was accompanied by the Tadcaster Drum and Fife band and a crowd of over 1,500 people. Mrs Levers was later dismissed after being found guilty of drunkenness, cruelty to the elderly inmates, and abuse of the children.

A new Tadcaster Union workhouse opened in 1872 on Station Road in Tadcaster (SE479431).

After 1930, the former workhouse became used as a geriatric hospital and later as an old people's home known as The Beeches. The building was demolished in 1987. (NRY)

THORNE

Thorne, Fishlake and Hatfield all had parish workhouses. In 1835, Thorne's was run by a contractor who was paid 2s 3d a week for each inmate of which there were thirty-one. Men worked in the workhouse's garden or on its 5 acres of land and fed its six pigs and cows.

In 1838, the new Thorne Union erected a workhouse on Poor House Road (later Union Road) at the west of Thorne (SE682132). The building broadly followed the popular cruciform layout. Later additions included a separate infirmary at the west of the site, and a casual block to the east.

Part of the main block survives and in recent years has been a base for the Sea Cadet Training Corps. The former infirmary has been used as a nursing home. (DON)

TODMORDEN

Todmorden and Walsden set up a canal-side workhouse at Gauxholme (SD930232) in 1801. Hepstonstall used a farm at Everhill Shaw (SD951295) until around 1810 then moved to Popples Bottom at Slack (SD977288). Other Heptonstall workhouses were at Langfield (Carr Green, SD951233), Midgley (New Heath Head, SE028268), Wadsworth (Spinks Hill, SD998305), and Stansfield (Blackshawhead).

Despite strong local opposition, Todmorden Poor Law Union was formed in February 1837. However, resistance to a new workhouse, led by local mill-owner John Fielden, held firm. Violent riots in November 1838 led to the calling-in of Dragoon Guards from Manchester. In 1844 the union was, exceptionally, given leave to abandon the requirement to provide a central workhouse. In 1847, three old workhouses at Gauxholme, Stansfield and Wadsworth were still in use.

Finally, in 1877, under threat of the union being dissolved, Todmorden became the last union in England to provide a proper workhouse when it erected one at Lee Bottom near Mankinholes (SD962238). Ironically, the site was on an estate known as Beggarington.

In 1930, the workhouse became a Public Assistance Institution. It then had 293 mostly elderly inmates, with sixty more in the infirmary. It later became Stansfield View Hospital and after 1948 provided care for the mentally handicapped. The buildings were demolished in 1996. (YWC)

WAKEFIELD

Wakefield's first poorhouse, linked to a House of Correction, opened in 1689. Another at Horbury was in use by 1747. By 1834, Wakefield had a workhouse on George Street (SE334206).

As elsewhere in Yorkshire, Wakefield opposed the New Poor Law and deterrent workhouse. In 1837, the new Board of Guardians retained the George Street workhouse. However, the building was regularly condemned for its squalor. In 1851, the *Wakefield Journal* reported that:

> In the females' day room there are several idiotic and also some insane girls and it is frequently the case that that girls of the town, full of loathsome disease, have to be sent into the house, but there is no separate place to put them in and they are left to mix with other inmates whom they contaminate by their obscene language and songs.

In 1851, a new workhouse for 300 inmates was erected on Park Lodge Lane (SE343207). The entrance buildings at the north contained the Master's offices, board-room, and casual wards. A central archway led to the T-shaped main block which housed males at the west and females at the east. Dining hall and kitchens were located to the rear.

In 1930, the site became Stanley View Public Assistance Institution, providing accommodation for the elderly and temporary housing for homeless families. The infirmary became Wakefield County Hospital also catering mainly for elderly patients. The site is now a housing estate. (YWW)

WETHERBY

A small poorhouse called Stone Dene existed on North Street in Wetherby. Another operated at Kirk Deighton (SE399502).

Wetherby Poor Law Union was created in February 1861. It was one of several new unions formed through the Poor Law Board's continuing efforts to unionize the West Riding, despite hindrance from the Gilbert Unions which still existed in the area.

Wetherby Union workhouse was built in 1863 on Linton Road in Wetherby (SE398484).

After 1930, the site became known as Wharfedale Lawn and provided care for elderly women and for the mentally handicapped. Under the NHS, it became Wharfe Grange Hospital, finally closing in January 1993. The site has now been redeveloped for residential use. (YWL)

WHARFEDALE

Like its neighbour Wetherby, the Wharfedale Poor Law Union was created in February 1861 as part of the slowly progressing unionization of the West Riding which had been obstructed by the continuing existence of the Carlton Gilbert Union.

In 1871, the union began construction of a new workhouse at Newall, north of Otley (SE199466). The buildings were constructed of local sandstone from the Farnley Hall estates. The entrance block, which faced onto Newall Carr Road, contained the board-room and vagrants' wards. Vagrants were not let in if they had any money or tobacco, so used to secrete any they had in cracks in a wall just outside the workhouse gates until their departure. In return for their lodging, vagrants mostly picked oakum (old ropes) whose fibres were then used to make mats.

In latter years, work for the permanent male inmates included the chopping up of old railway sleepers into firewood which was then sold to the public and delivered on hand-carts.

In 1930, the workhouse was taken over by the local council and became known as Otley County Hospital, later Wharfedale General Hospital. The hospital's relocation to an adjacent site in 2004 left the old buildings, now listed, standing empty (YWL)

WORTLEY

In the 1770s, workhouses were in operation at Wortley, Bradfield and Ecclesfield. The Wortley workhouse was at Finkle Street to the south-west of the town (SK303989). Bradfield's workhouse stood at the centre of Upper (or High) Bradfield (SK268926). In the 1730s, Ecclesfield erected

The main block of Wetherby Union workhouse had the Master's quarters at the centre, with male accommodation to the north, and female to the south. Small casual wards were located to each side.

The main building of Wharfedale Union workhouse was over 150 feet long, with a clock tower over its entrance. Aged and infirm inmates occupied the front of the building, with the able-bodied at the rear, and children at the far end of each side. To the rear were the kitchen and the dining hall which originally also served as a chapel.

The former entrance and administrative block is the last surviving part of the Wortley Union workhouse.

a workhouse known as the Feoffees Hall at the west of St Mary's Lane (SK354940). Another workhouse may have stood on Bower Lane at Grenoside (SK330941).

In 1839 Wortley was noted as one of the unions which 'for the present decline to concur in providing an adequate workhouse' although the old local workhouses continued in use.

In 1850-52, a new workhouse was built on Salt Box Lane at Grenoside (SK335934) designed by Aicken & Capes. The main block had a cruciform layout with Master's quarters and dining-hall at the north, male accommodation at the west, and female at the east. A hospital block was located at the north-west of the site and a porters' lodge and board-room at the north facing onto the road. A casuals' block and labour yard stood on the opposite side of Salt Box Lane.

The site is now used for residential care. Virtually all the old buildings have been demolished. (SHE)

WORKHOUSE RECORDS

Poor Law related records prior to 1834 include:

Parish Overseers' Accounts – listing poor rates collected and allowances paid
Churchwardens' Accounts – listing work done on the church and church-owned houses
Vestry Minutes – general administration of parish matters, sometimes including poorhouses
Settlement Records – settlement certificates, settlement examinations, and removal orders
Corporate Records – records of Poor Law Incorporations, Gilbert Unions etc.

The Poor Law Commission, established by the 1834 Poor Law Act, created a vast bureaucratic machine. It issued a continual stream of orders and regulations, and conducted voluminous correspondence with each of the 600 or so unions, each of which was required to consult with the Commissioners about a whole range of issues. Union and workhouse officers were required to maintain a large number of records – one 1860s catalogue listed over 130 books and forms for the use of union clerks, relieving officers, medical officers, and workhouse Masters. These include:

- *Admission and Discharge Book* – with details of each admitted and departing inmate.
- *Admission and Discharge of Casuals* – recording the name of the vagrant and his family, where he slept the previous night, work done, and next destination.
- *Porter's Book* – records the names of all persons entering or leaving the workhouse premises, including inmates, union officers and other officials, tradesmen, etc.
- *Indoor Relief List* – giving a parish-by-parish summary of every inmate's length of stay.
- *Creed Register* – (from 1869) details of each inmate's religious creed, and date of admission/discharge. Sometimes includes occupation, last address, and next of kin.
- *Register of Births* – with dates of birth and baptism, and name of parents or mother.
- *Register of Baptisms* – (where a workhouse had its own chapel).
- *Register of Deaths* – with age, place of burial, and parish chargeable.
- *Register of Burials* – (where a union had its own burial ground).
- *Workhouse Punishment Book* – with details of each offence and the punishment received.
- *Workhouse Medical Relief Book* – with the name, illness, and dietary of each inmate treated.
- *Clothing Register Book* – a record of the numbered uniform issued to each inmate.
- *Register of Inmates' Own Clothing*
- *Register of Attendance at Workhouse School* – including the name and age of each pupil.
- *Board of Guardians' Minutes* – the record of the weekly Guardians' meetings. The contents are largely financial matters but individual inmates occasionally feature.

The survival of records varies widely. In some cases, for example Oldham Union, a wide variety of records survives. In others, such as Toxteth Park, virtually no local records exist. Records have been lost for many reasons. In some cases, they were pulped to produce paper, as part of a wartime salvage drive. In others, they were deliberately disposed of as being of no interest, or as an unwanted reminder of former times.

The main location of locally held records is indicated at the end of each union's entry in the workhouse directory – further details are given in the next section.

In addition, the UK National Archives at Kew in Surrey holds the archives of the Poor Law Commissioners, and their successors the Poor Law Board, the Local Government Board, and the Ministry of Health. The three main categories of archive at Kew are correspondence with poor law unions, workhouse staff lists and workhouse plans.

RECORD REPOSITORIES

Below are the website addresses of record offices for the areas covered in this book, in order of the code given at the end of each directory entry. If no website exists, a postal address is given.

BAR	Barnsley Archives – www.barnsley.gov.uk/archives
BOL	Bolton Archives – www.boltonmuseums.org.uk/bolton-archives
BRY	Bury Archive Service – www.bury.gov.uk/archives
CUB	Cumbria Record Office (Barrow) – www.cumbria.gov.uk/archives/recordoffices/barec.asp
CUC	Cumbria Record Office (Carlisle) – www.cumbria.gov.uk/archives/recordoffices/carec.asp
CUK	Cumbria Record Office (Kendal) – www.cumbria.gov.uk/archives/recordoffices/knrec.asp
CUW	Cumbria Record Office (Whitehaven) – www.cumbria.gov.uk/archives/recordoffices/whrec.asp
DON	Doncaster Archives – www.doncaster.gov.uk/Services/Archives.asp
DUR	Durham County Record Office – www.durham.gov.uk/recordoffice
HUL	Hull History Centre – www.hullhistorycentre.org.uk
KEI	Keighley Reference Library, North Street, Keighley, BD2 1 3SX
LAN	Lancashire Record Office, Preston – www.lancashire.gov.uk/education/record_office
LIV	Liverpool Record Office – www.liverpool.gov.uk/archives
MAN	Greater Manchester Record Office – www.manchester.gov.uk/libraries/arls
NON	No locally held records are known to survive.
NOR	Northumberland Collections Service – www.northumberland.gov.uk/collections
OLD	Oldham Local Studies and Archives – www.oldham.gov.uk/community/local_studies
SHE	Sheffield Archives – www.sheffield.gov.uk/libraries/archives-and-local-studies
ROT	Rotherham Archives – www.rotherham.gov.uk/graphics/Learning/Archives
TAM	Tameside Local Studies and Archives – www.tameside.gov.uk/localstudies
TAW	Tyne & Wear Archives – www.tyneandweararchives.org.uk
TSD	Teesside Archives – www.teessidearchives.middlesbrough.gov.uk/calmview
WIG	Wigan Archive Service – www.wlct.org/heritage-services/wigan-archives-service.htm
YER	East Riding Archives, Beverley – www.eastriding.gov.uk/leisure/archives-family-and-local-history
YNR	North Yorkshire County Record Office, Northallerton – www.northyorks.gov.uk/archives
YRK	York City Archives – www.york.gov.uk/leisure/archives
YWB	West Yorkshire Archives, Bradford – www.archives.wyjs.org.uk/archives-calderdale.asp
YWC	West Yorkshire Archives, Halifax – www.archives.wyjs.org.uk/ablocc.html
YWK	West Yorkshire Archives, Huddersfield – www.archives.wyjs.org.uk/achives-huddersfield.asp
YWL	West Yorkshire Archives, Leeds – www.archives.wyjs.org.uk/archives-leeds.asp
YWW	West Yorkshire Archives, Wakefield – www.archives.wyjs.org.uk/archives-wakefield.asp

Web addresses can change over time. Where this has happened, enter the record office name into a search engine, or search the relevant local authority web pages (e.g. *www.cumbria.gov.uk*) for 'archives' or 'records' in their A-Z directory.

Before travelling any distance to visit a record office, always check that the records you want are available for consultation. Records containing personal details often have restricted access for a hundred years from the latest entry in a particular volume.

Workhouses also feature in the ten-yearly UK censuses, which are increasingly available for searching online, for example at *http://www.nationalarchives.gov.uk/census*

FURTHER READING

My website *www.workhouses.org.uk* contains further information on all the workhouses mentioned in this book and elsewhere in the British Isles.

Anonymous (1732) *An Account of Several Work-houses for Employing and Maintaining the Poor.*
Bedford, P. and Howard, D.N., (1989) *St James' Hospital, Leeds.*
Bowen, J.M. (2005) *A Poor Little House: The Story of Belford Union Workhouse.*
Chadwick, A. (1996) [Leaflets on Yorkshire workhouses published by Ripon Museums Trust].
Cole, J. (1984) *Down Poorhouse Lane – the Diary of a Rochdale Workhouse.*
Connor, B. (1989) *A Pauper's Palace: A History of Fishpool Institution.* [Bolton workhouse].
Crowther, M.A. (1978) *The Workhouse System 1834-1929.*
Drinkall, M. (2009) *Rotherham Workhouse*
Drinkall, M. (2011) *Sheffield Workhouse*
Driver, F. (1993) *Power and Pauperism: The Workhouse System, 1834-1884.*
Eden, Sir Frederic Morton (1797) *The State of the Poor.*
Edwards, Gerard (1975) *The Road to Barlow Moor.* [Chorlton Union]
Fallowfield, M. and Watson, I. (1985) *The New Poor Law in Humberside.*
Flett, Joan (1984) *The Story of the Workhouse and the Hospital at Nether Edge.*
Forrest, D. (2001) *Warrington's Poor and the Workhouse.*
Gibson, J. and Rogers, C. (2008) *Poor Law Union Records: 2. The Midlands and Northern England.*
Hall, Susan (2004) *Workhouses and Hospitals of North Manchester.*
Hastings, R.P. (1996) [Leaflets on Yorkshire workhouses published by Ripon Museums Trust]
Ibid. (1982) 'Poverty and the Poor law in the North Riding of Yorkshire *c.* 1780-1837', *Borthwick Institute Papers* No. 61.
Higginbotham, P. (2008) *The Workhouse Cookbook*
Howsam, L. (2004) *A Child's Life in Gawber Road Workhouse.* [Barnsley Union]
Hemingway, J. (1831) *History of the City of Chester.*
Kitts, J. (1909) 'The Poor Laws with Special Reference to the Old Sunderland Workhouses', *Antiquities of Sunderland and its Vicinity* (X, 133-151).
Knott, J. (1986) *Popular Opposition to the 1834 Poor Law.*
Leonard, E.M. (1965) *The Early History of English Poor Relief.*
Longmate, N. (2004) *The Workhouse.*
Lofthouse, F. (2001) *Keepers of the House.* [Clitheroe Union]
Hurrell, G. and Harlan, G.P. (1996) *The History of Newcastle General Hospital.*
Midwinter, E.C. (1969) *Social Administration in Lancashire 1830-1860.*
Morrison, Kathryn (1999) *The Workhouse – a Study of Poor Law Buildings in England.*
Pennock, P. (1986) 'The Evolution of St James's 1845-94', *Thoresby Society* (LIX, Part 2, No. 130, 129-176).
Place, Allan (2004) *Pray Remember the Poor: The Poor Laws and Huddersfield.*
Proctor, W. (1965) 'Poor Law Administration in Preston Union 1838-1948', *Trans. Hist. Soc. Lancs. & Cheshire*, 117, 145-166.
Reid, D.S. (ed.) (1981) *Durham Under the Old Poor Law.*
Thompson, R.N. (1978) 'The Working of the Poor Law Amendment Act in Cumbria, 1836-1871', *Northern History* (XIV, 119-137).
Whitehead, J. (2006) *Lost Children: Ulverston Workhouse in the 19th Century.*

Other local titles published by The History Press

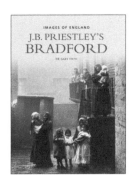

J.B. Priestley's Bradford
GARY FIRTH

This book examines the influences of Edwardian Bradford which were at work upon the author in his formative years. We are given an insight into the pre-First World War Bradford way of life in which Gary Firth reveals a vivid, if transient, understanding of a great writer's 'lost world' – and so it was, for Priestley's early life coincided with the zenith of Bradford's golden age as a classic nineteenth-century provincial town.

0-7524-3865-4

Madmen
ROY PORTER

Best-selling popular historian Roy Porter looks at the bizarre and savage practices of early doctors for treating those afflicted by 'manias', ranging from huge doses of opium, blood-letting and cold water immersion to beatings, confinement in cages and blistering. The author also reveals how the London asylum Bethlem was riddled with sadism and embezzlement, and that sightseers were permitted entry – *for a fee of course.*

0-7524-3730-5

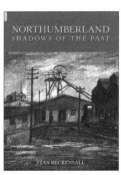

Northumberland Shadows of the Past
STAN BECKENSALL

This work examines the outward and visible survivals in the landscape that help to explain the events of history. It includes such diverse signs as fossils, ancient and recent agricultural landscapes, abandoned transport systems and the remnants of an industrial past. Monumental inscriptions and documentary sources are used to illuminate conditions in Northumberland towns, showing how people lived, how they died and what they believed.

0-7524-3347-4

Brass Castles
GEORGE SHEERAN

The West Yorkshire families who grew rich through commerce and industry during the Industrial Revolution used their newly acquired wealth to build houses and gardens that were markedly different from those of older landed and commercial families. In this fascinating sociological approach to architectural history, George Sheeran examines the urban as well as the rural homes of ninety-two of the wealthiest families from the 'New Rich' section of the population in the period 1800-1914.

0-7524-3806-9

If you are interested in purchasing other books published by The History Press, or in case you have difficulty finding any of our books in your local bookshop, you can also place orders directly through our website

www.thehistorypress.co.uk